INTERCULTURAL SOURCEBOOK

CROSS-CULTURAL TRAINING METHODOLOGIES

DAVID S. HOOPES

PAUL VENTURA

Editors

THE SOCIETY FOR INTERCULTURAL EDUCATION, TRAINING AND RESEARCH
1414 22nd Street, Washington, D.C., 20037

Published and Distributed by

Intercultural Press, Inc.
70 W. Hubbard Street
Chicago, Illinois 60610

1979

This publication is part of a large scale project to study the state of intercultural education, training and research directed by George Renwick. Funding for the project has been contributed by the Bureau of Educational and Cultural Affairs, U.S. Department of State (now Directorate, Educational and Cultural Affairs, U.S. International Communication Agency); the Bilingual Bicultural Education Department, Illinois Office of Education; the Office of Naval Research; the Kettering Foundation of Ohio; and the Society for Intercultural Education, Training and Research.

Library of Congress Catalogue Card Number: 79-83667

ISBN 0-933662-00-9

Second Printing, August 1980

Printed in the United States of America

INTERCULTURAL SOURCEBOOK:

CROSS-CULTURAL TRAINING METHODOLOGIES

TABLE OF CONTENTS

CHAPTER

CHAPTER

*　*　*　*　*

PREFACE

This volume is part of the SIETAR Project to Study the State of Intercultural Education Training and Research. It was felt that one of the results of this study should be a compilation of the best materials and information we have on cross-cultural training. It is our experience that people working in the intercultural field have a crying need for such materials and information. It is hoped this volume will take a concrete step in meeting that need.

In it we have tried to survey the principal forms of cross-cultural training and have been guided in our selection of methodologies by the following objectives:

(1) The identification of materials not easily available in other published form;

(2) the presentation of materials in a usable format for incorporation in teaching/training programs;

(3) the inclusion of materials of a more theoretical nature in order to clarify the learning principles behind given methodologies; and finally,

(4) the desire to be as comprehensive as possible by including samples of the most familiar methods (simulations, for instance), as well as some of the lesser known, but nonetheless valuable, approaches (such a self-guided study).

Further, we have been motivated to provide not just training materials, but insights into the nature of the training process and how learning materials may be created and used most effectively. In achieving this we have not hesitated to include both complex analyses of training methods (the contrast-American, for instance) and simple guidelines to the use of basic exercises. Cross-cultural training is not yet so fragmented as to have produced narrow specializations. Each of us must deal with the training process on a multiplicity of levels. We are trainers of all trades.

For most of the activities included herein, we have omitted the usual precautionary notes regarding their use. Suffice it to say that anyone conducting such experiences should be thoroughly familiar with

1

the exercise or format used, be satisfied as to its appropriateness for the individual or group, and should establish provisions for the adequate discussion and processing of each experience. More than anything else, however, the facilitator/trainer must have an abiding respect for and a sense of personal responsibility toward the group. Only with these can true learning occur.

Our thanks go to many people, especially to George Renwick, the Associate Director of the Project, who assiduously gathered materials for inclusion in this volume, and to the many, many others who generously responded by sending materials to us.

We wish finally to express our appreciation for the faith and patience which have been demonstrated by our associates in the Department of State's Bureau of Educational and Cultural Affairs (now the Directorate of Educational and Cultural Affairs of the International Communications Agency) and the Governing Council and members of SIETAR.

David S. Hoopes
Paul Ventura

INTRODUCTION:

Notes on the Evolution of Cross-Cultural Training

In December 1975, I was invited to a five-day conference/workshop in Bonn, Germany, sponsored by the German Foundation for International Development (the German AID). Its aim was to bring together European and North American directors of cross-cultural training to explore subjects of mutual interest. Nine countries and about fifteen, mostly governmental, organizations and agencies, including the Canadian International Development Agency and the World Bank, were represented. (The most prominent absentee was the Peace Corps.) The meeting was valuable in a number of ways, but one of the most striking things we learned that week was that every training director there had progressed along an almost identical route in developing his methodological approaches to cross-cultural training.

The figure below illustrates the evolution of cross-cultural training approaches as experienced by the Bonn training directors:

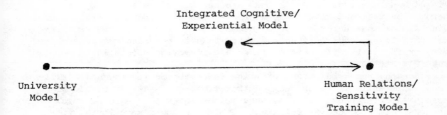

All at some point in time had more or less suddenly been asked to prepare technicians or volunteers for service overseas. All knew that there was an important cultural dimension to the training they were being called upon to provide, yet few had significant experience as cross-cultural trainers. They turned first, quite logically, to traditional education for their model. They sat trainees down in classrooms and

3

presented information to them about the target country and culture. It was not long, however, before word began to seep back from the field (then deluge them during the debriefing of returnees) that the "university model" of cross-cultural training they were using left the trainees largely unprepared for the realities of functioning in a radically different socio-cultural environment. Skills in communication and cross-cultural adjustment turned out to be as much or more important than country-specific information. Perhaps even more significant was the dawning recognition that becoming effective overseas involved a heavy measure of self-understanding and awareness.

What resulted was the rapid progress along a spectrum from cognitive, information-oriented training programs to those oriented toward experiential learning and "personal growth."

This occurred during the decade of the 1960s when human relations or sensitivity training had achieved a peak of acceptance. It had been used extensively in business and was soon to become pervasive in education. The National Training Laboratories was a large, thriving, and influential organization. A number of universities were training PhD's in "organizational behavior." Publications on the subject were appearing with increasing frequency.

Faced with the need to deal with behaviors and attitudes rooted in unconscious values and cultural traditions, the training directors uniformly turned to human relations training--and in almost every case got severely burned. This was particularly true where participation in the training was not wholly voluntary. The response of many trainees was strongly negative. Inadequately prepared trainers induced psychological stress with which they were not able to deal. Occasionally a relatively severe psychological breakdown marred the training program.

In addition it soon became apparent that while the communication and self-awareness skills which resulted from human relations training were of some relevance and value overseas, there were major deficiencies in the methodology. First, human relations training spawns its own behavioral and attitudinal norms that are no more universal than any others. The frequent result was a cross-cultural blindness hardly less dysfunctional than unregenerate ethnocentrism. Such qualities as openness, directness, confrontiveness, which tend to become norms in sensitivity training, translate into biases and stumbling blocks in the encounter with contrasting cultures.

Second, human relations training too often failed to deal directly and substantively with such central cross-cultural issues as perceptual differences, cultural assumptions and values, and cultural awareness. It produced self-insight within the American cultural context, but it did not consistently result in self-awareness in cross-cultural situations. Finally, from the cross-cultural perspective, human relations training suffered the same shortcoming it did elsewhere --it tended to be so thoroughly experiential that it left participants without a conceptual framework within which to turn it into a usable tool. In the end, for most people, the benefit lay in a behavioral residue rather than in a cognitively integrated self-management skill.

Stung by sensitivity training, the training directors beat a hasty retreat. The Peace Corps was a classic example. The reaction

4

to sensitivity training was traumatic. Jack Vaughn banned it with
such stringency that for some time all experiential cross-cultural
training in the Peace Corps came under a cloud. But a return to the
classroom was not the answer. The profession, which was beginning by
this time--the early seventies--to emerge as such, searched for methods
more precisely suited to the special and complex needs of cross-cultural training. There were several important dimensions to this search.
First, the training domain, or the target area within the individual,
had to be more clearly defined. A distinction had to be made between
culture and personality, with the former identified as the proper domain of cross-cultural training--and the latter left to qualified
psychotherapists. Second, a more effective means of integrating cognitive and experiential learning had to be found. The indeterminate
"feelings" left over from sensitivy or purely experiential training
were inadequate to the development of needed cross-cultural skills.

Increasingly trainers experimented with methods which, while
tapping into trainee feelings and bringing unconscious cultural attitudes and values to the surface, stopped short of penetrating deeply
into emotions and personality structures. At the same time, more attention was paid to the theoretical framework of intercultural communication and cross-cultural human relations so that cognition and experience
were joined effectively in the training process.

The outcome has been the elaboration and refinement of the
methodologies represented in this Sourcebook. These training approaches are designed to help the trainee experience or encounter perceptual
and value differences, respond to them, and integrate the resultant
learning into their own patterns of thinking and behaving.

There is still a long way to go. The methods need further refinement. They have not been sufficiently evaluated. Cross-cultural
training still remains unsystematized. But these will come. The important thing is that all the evidence indicates that we are now on the
right track.

David S. Hoopes

Vershire, Vermont
December, 1978

CHAPTER I

ROLE-PLAYING

ROLE-PLAYING

Paula Barnak

Description

Role-playing as a training process is really <u>reality practice</u> or <u>role practice</u>. It is people simulating real-life behavior, given a familiar or non-familiar role. The participants in a role-play improvise their script as they go along and the "make-believe" situation is acted out as if it were "real." Many different role-playing situations can be developed covering various aspects of experience with the host nationals and their customs (instructional situations, counseling situations, informal and formal social relations, etc.).

Purpose

Role-playing can help participants develop a better understanding of their role in various intercultural situations they might encounter. It can be used as a method for learning about host national customs and for practicing behavorial and verbal dialogues with host nationals. It has also proved effective for promoting real attitude change.

Role-playing as a training technique can effectively accomplish or facilitate the following more specific objectives:

- To provide practice in intercultural communication skills.

- To provide practice in the execution of individual actions or solutions.

- To explore situations in which the reactions and feelings of individuals are involved.

- To stimulate participation and involvement.

- To develop a better understanding of the points of view of others.

Development

Role-playing situations can arise <u>spontaneously</u> out of content being discussed or can be <u>structured</u> to achieve specific objectives. A spontaneous role-play can often arise out of a discussion of a critical incident. To illustrate and practice different solutions to an incident, you (the trainer) might play the role of the host national and ask a participant to play himself and to respond spontaneously with what he would do in this situation. Other trainees can be asked what they would do, and their responses compared. (If any trainee seems significantly confident, he could be asked to play the host national and another to play the second part.)

In developing situations beforehand (structured role-playing), you must first assess the specific objectives you want to achieve. For instance, one of your objectives might be to interpret and respond to non-verbal behavior. You must choose the appropriate non-verbal signals (American or foreign) and then focus the situation on how and when to engage in these behaviors. Content for role-playing situations can be obtained from trainees' past experiences and from interviews with host nationals.

7

Format

The following is an example of instructions for a role-playing situation in non-verbal behavior involving a total group of participants:

Instructions for Members of an "Unspecified" Cultural Group

In a 2- to 3-minute discussion of how you (the foreign nationals) are getting along in America, engage in the following non-verbal gestures:

1. When introducing yourself to the American, pump his hand 10 times while shaking hands.
2. Hold your head 6 inches closer to the person you are speaking to than you normally would.
3. Touch for emphasis; put your hand on his shoulder or put your arm around him (even same sex) while talking.
4. Exaggerate your hand movements.
5. Use your chin to point.
6. Use the so-called "Latin shrug" (shoulder movements).
7. Don't look the person in the eyes (look down) while talking.
8. Talk very fast and raise your voice as your excitement grows.
9. "Blink" your nose to ask "What?"
10. "Move" to express disapproval or annoyance.

Instructions for the "American" Group

In a 2- to 3-minute discussion of how the "foreign nationals" are getting along in America, they will engage in non-verbal gestures that are common among people from many different countries.

Procedures

Although role-playing is an effective training technique, it is complex and involves trainer skills and establishing trust within the training group. Structured role-playing must be carefully <u>planned</u>, <u>introduced</u>, <u>ended</u>, and <u>evaluated</u>.

Planning

1. Role-playing should be appropriate to the group objectives and to the trainer. It should be used only if and when it will be useful, not just for the sake of doing it or to show off a new trick.

2. The role-playing situation should present a valid problem in cross-cultural attitudes and communication, and be relevant to the trainees' current or future responsibilities.

3. Once you have chosen the role-playing situations, write out a description of the roles and scenes for the role players.

- Make the roles understood by avoiding long complex sentences and unnecessary facts and data.

- Describe each role in a manner which will allow the trainee to identify with the role. Establish the identity in the first sentence. Use the second person "you" in writing the role-play.

- Write the role-play to allow creative and individual responses. Describe the apparent behavior but avoid moralistic description of it (lazy, greedy, dishonest, etc.) State the problem, but do not state how to handle the problem.

- Write the roles to focus trainees on the process rather than the content. Avoid situations which may involve digressions into complicated technical problems.

- Include conflicting motivations which may result from cultural values, perceptual differences, divergent goals, and procedures which are necessitated by the work process. For example, the case of foreign officers cleaning their rooms, cleaning the ship, or standing watch.

4. In your planning ask yourself:

- How can the material be introduced most effectively?

- How can the group be aided to achieve the greatest possible insight?

- What can be done to help those playing roles, and those who are watching, to feel "at home" in their respective activities?

Introducing the Role-Play

1. Sensitize the group to the need to work on a particular problem.

2. Get action started naturally without belaboring the technique as "role-playing."

3. Be sensitive to interpersonal relationships within the group.

4. Weigh the value of taking part yourself or acting only as discussion leader. (If there is group hesitation, you may opt to play one of the roles as a model and to obtain group trust.)

5. In assigning roles, any of the following methods may be used:

- Ask participants to volunteer for specific roles.

- Ask group to suggest which member should take each role.

- Role may be defined so clearly that only one person can identify with the role.

Implementing the Exercise

1. Warm up the cast by allowing time for each role-player to read and understand the role.

9

2. Allow role-players to set up tables and chairs as they like, and to leave the room and start role-playing on re-entering.

3. Help the audience to observe more skillfully by:

   - Giving them something specific to watch for (e.g., What was the host national's response to the American's action? What do you think of the handling of the problem by the American? Why did the players act as they did?)

   - Asking them to note special actions or responses to discuss later.

   - Distributing clue-sheets to be used in later discussion.

Ending the Scene

Do not allow the scene to go beyond the crisis point since everyone will get restless and digressions will begin.

Evaluating

1. Every role-play should be followed by a debriefing or evaluative discussion.

2. First, ask each role-player how he or she felt about what happened.

3. Then ask how the group felt about what happened.

   - Why do you feel the players acted the way they did?

   - What do you think of the solutions proposed?

   - What other solutions do you think might work?

4. Replay the scene, using same or different players, to try a new approach to the problem.

Excerpted with permission from: Iceland Defense Force (IDF) Overseas Diplomacy Program, Vol. II, "Overseas Diplomacy Training Program Manual." Center for Research and Education, Denver, Colorado, May 1976.

ROLE-PLAYS

Henry Holmes and Stephen Guild

   Introduction: Role-plays are avoided by many teachers because
of a certain mystique which has grown up around this technique. Much
of the awe is unjustified, but in order to make the role play a
successful learning technique, the trainer needs to understand the
purposes of the method and the careful preparations required.
   Role playing can be an extremely effective technique for having
participants experience, at first hand, many of the cultural principles
which up to this moment they may have only read or discussed in fairly
abstract terms. It is a chance to translate these ideas into action.
During the role play, participants must practice social skills appropriate
to a realistic situation, even as their valued ideas are being tested
against someone else's from another culture. Especially valuable is
the opportunity for participants to be emotionally (as well as intellectually) involved in inter-cultural learning, and to be able to reflect
on the experience.
   As a basis for role playing, it is essential that participants
first have some fairly solid background about the culture and the
people before they will be able to feel at home in a role. Although
they could act out a scene during the early stages of the learning
program, much of the acting at that point would be based on guesswork.
It is preferable, then, to use role playing as a kind of capstone to
the entire program, where a person can demonstrate his ability to use
what he knows and apply his cultural skills.

   Procedure:
1. The leader should review program materials and experiences and,
    if possible, discuss with members of the culture being studied,
    any major cultural differences which might constitute an effective
    role play. He might ask for specific examples the respondents have
    observed in which members of another culture have come in contact
    with their own-- at the market, school, customs office, or
    social visits. Still better, identify an encounter which the
    training group members themselves might expect to face when they
    visit the unfamiliar community.

2. The trainer-leader then prepares some objectives, based partly on
    material previously learned and partly on goals which only the
    role play can offer, for example:

    a. Demonstrate an understanding of the importance of conformity
        and tradition;

11

    b.   Demonstrate an understanding of the value of status and respect for authority;

    c.   Show an awareness of different attitudes toward change and other foreign values;

    d.   Show skill in dealing with an official from another culture;

    e.   Show awareness of certain family pressures faced by the other person;

    f.   Demonstrate the ability to control one's own tendency to push one's own point of view; find a thoughtful compromise, and control one's frustration during the process.

3.   From this information the leader composes a single incident on which to build the role play. It should be a short encounter which can be "played out" in 15 or 20 minutes.

4.   The leader writes a one-paragraph general statement describing the scene (a "Scenario") for the actors and the observers.

5.   He prepares short written "instructions" for the two or three participants who are to join the role play. The instructions should be a paragraph or two in length and sufficiently sketchy to allow a great deal of freedom in interpretation. Each character's point of view toward the encounter should be described in positive terms, so that each appears to be logical in its cultural context. But the roles should be directed

    a.   toward conflicting ends or

    b.   by means which are not compatible

The issues and disagreements will arise from the various perceptions of reality viewed through the experience of each character.

6.   The size of the group is important. Besides the actors, there should not be more than 6 observers, for fear that the actors may be distracted from their own encounter.

7.   At the beginning of the session, it is especially important to try to involve all the participants, including observers, in the activity.

    a.   Begin the session by saying to everyone that in a moment two of them will be chosen to play roles based on the scenario about to be handed out. "Two of you will be sitting in those two chairs".

    b.   Give them a few minutes to read the scenario and discuss how they would approach each role if they were chosen to act in it.

    c.   Select two members to play the roles; do not necessarily choose those who will "perform best" in the roles, but two who can benefit themselves and the observers by participating.

    d.   Ask the remaining members, as they are breathing sighs of relief, to prepare to make observations on a number of points: The sources of conflict between the characters, differences in behavior (spoken and unspoken), and feelings shown during the action.

After the scene has been played, allow 20 to 30 minutes for discussion of it. Sample questions:

1. What was each of the people trying to accomplish?
2. Where did the problems lie?
3. What differences did you notice in how each one behaved in carrying out their task? What non-verbal differences did you see?
4. To what extent was the behavior of each person suitable to his task? How effective was he?
5. How do you think each one _felt_ during the conversation? How could you tell?
6. How might _you_ have approached (either) role?

Turning finally to the actors, each one is asked to describe: 1) how he _felt_ during the session and, 2) how he might have conducted himself in order to feel more comfortable and/or effective.

Be sure to tie the role play, by way of summary, to the various other activities of the inter-cultural program. All participants were asked to take a few minutes to record what they learned from the session; optionally, they may volunteer to tell the group any points they have written down.

Variations:

1. Use a member of the community being studied as one of the actors.
2. Select new actors from among the observers and run through the role play again.
3. Use video tape equipment to record the action. Play it back to the group to illustrate and study particularly important gestures or issues which arose.

SAMPLE ROLE PLAY

Scenario:

A girl of 17 has been able to visit a foreign country for the first time this summer, through her own savings and some help from her parents. She is fortunate that one of her former school chums, a boy named Sim, lives in the capital and has invited her to stay with him and his family.

Now that she has been a guest with Sim's family for a week, it is time to get an extension of her visa so she can stay longer. She appears at the Immigration Office with her passport, expecting to meet with one of the Imigration Officers.

The Student: Role A

Today is the last day for obtaining an extension to your visa. You regret having to spend half the day in a government office, especially since Sim's family was hoping to take you to a local festival. You have heard about red tape and inefficiency in countries like these. You hope the visa won't take too long so you can enjoy the rest of the day.

The Official: Role B

You have held this immigration job for several years now. Much of the work is routine. Lately, your government has been concerned

about the large numbers of young people from western countries who
have come here to visit. Many of them, because of their sloppy
dress and long hair, are considered a bad influence on our local
customs. Some officials think that they introduce drugs and other
bad habits to our young people.

You enjoy talking to young people, especially from European
countries. It helps you practice your English. As you talk to
this young woman, you discover she is here on her own and visiting
a local young man here in the capital. This is not the usual thing
for a young girl. If she is not a proper girl, her application would
present a problem. Besides, visa applications sometimes take time.

YOU ARE TO ACT EXACTLY AS THOUGH THIS WERE A REAL SITUATION.
YOU MAY SAY OR DO ANYTHING YOU FEEL WILL BE APPROPRIATE.

Reprinted with permission from Henry Holmes and Stephen Guild, Manual
of Teaching Techniques for Intercultural Education, University of
Massachusetts, Amherst, 1971.

SITUATIONAL EXERCISES

Henry Holmes and Stephen Guild

General Description. This is essentially a short, free-form
skit, partially written in advance, using one or more "actors" who
have had time to rehearse their parts. It is similar to role-
play, but does not require the participants to behave in a certain
way as role-play does.

The student is given only a general description of the setting,
and he must rely on his knowledge of the culture and his wits as
he thinks and acts on his feet in an unfamiliar situation. The
"actors" need to be people of some self-confidence who will help
move the situation along. Foreign students willing to participate
would be the best "actors", but this may not always be possible.
Good planning is a must for the success of situational exercises.

Group Size. There is no particular group size, but it would
be difficult to have a successful situational exercise in a class
larger than 25-30, since the participants may feel threatened by
a large group.

Time Required. No particular time. Situational exercises can
be done in 2-5 minutes or can run 20-30 minutes, depending upon the
situation and the participants. One class period would be sufficient.

Materials Utilized. 1. Scenario. 2. Individual Roles.
3. Props (dress, artifacts, etc.).

Physical Setting. Any standard classroom. One with moveable
chairs is most suitable.

Process. The initial steps in setting up situational exercises
are similiar to those of constructing a role play. A scenario should
be decided upon, roles constructed and written out and, when possible,con-
sultation   with someone of that culture to check out the details.
The situation should be constructed to highlight the differences between the culture being studied and the students' own backgrounds,
and should pose, implicitly, some problem needing resolution (a 'white'
youth in a 'black' home, a Westerner in another country, etc.).

1. Distribute the scenario to the entire class, who will be observers. This is the only information they will receive.

2. Distribute the roles and a scenario to the "actors" being careful not to expose one role to the other.

3. Set the stage both physically--with props, furniture, etc.-- and educationally by preparing the observers and participants for what they are going to do. (There is a tendency, especially at first, to treat role plays and situational exercises lightly, so the teacher's role is very important in setting the right mood.)

4. When all are clear on their parts, start the exercise. Let it run as long as you feel it is productive, but generally when things begin to lag, it should be stopped.

5. Follow with discusssion, perhaps 20-30 minutes, organized around these suggested topics:

   a. What was each of the individuals trying to accomplish?
   b. What were the problems?
   c. What differences did you notice in each individual's behavior? What non-verbal differences did you observe?
   d. How do you think each felt during the scene?

6. After observers have shared their ideas on these, allow the participants to give their own reactions to the same points.

Special Instructions. Care must be taken in writing the situation so it is believable--and performable. You might have to try several situations before you get the right one. Be sure that the scenario is written as non-value-laden as possible. It should be a simple description of the facts and should not bias the reader one way or the other. Make sure the roles are clear and descriptive, but do not make them so rigid that the participants have no freedom of action.

Try as hard as possible to check the accuracy of the exercise before conducting it. This is a powerful teaching device and stereotypes and inaccuracies are often exaggerated with these types of methods.

When selecting a student for the situational exercises, do not necessarily choose the one who will "perform" the best, but one who can benefit personally from the experience.

This exercise could be used again with an observer, and even though he would have more information and benefit from the first students' participation, the exercise can still be a valuable comparative tool.

If video-tape equipment is available, the entire exercise can be recorded and then played back immediately or at a later time.

Resources.

Wright, Albert R. and Mary Anne Hammons. Guidelines ror Peace Corps Cross-Cultural Training. Estes Park, Colorado: Center for Research and Education; or Washington, D.C., Peace Corps, Office of Training Support, 1970.

A Situational Exercise

The Situation: A Tutoring Project. Because it is a large
urban school serving a somewhat unstable population, Bourdin School
has found it difficult to maintain close relations with members of
the community. One particular aspect of this problem is the increasing number of immigrants to the community from different ethnic and
racial backgrounds whose children are often very unprepared--from
a cultural and language standpoint--for the academic and social
expectations of the school.

The principal, in an effort to improve the school's service to
the community, set to work with members of the English department
and student leaders and introduced a program whereby older student
volunteers would offer tutoring to younger children from immigrant
families. These lessons would be given in the family's home. The
school hoped that the service would result in more rapid adjustment
to school life for the new student and increased confidence in the
school on the part of the new parents. It might also offer a good
cultural experience for the tutor.

Mee Loon is 15. Her parents have very recently emigrated
from Hong Kong. Her English teacher at Bourdin, observing her
difficulty with English, recommended to her the student tutoring
service, and suggested she explain about it to her parents. If
they agreed to the sessions, the school would select a student
to come to the house and arrange a tutoring schedule suitable to
the family.

John, a 17-year-old student in his final year of secondary
school, was told yesterday that the parents of a Chinese girl,
Mee Loon, were interested in someone to tutor her English. John
agreed to visit the house which was located in the Chinatown district, and start tutoring her as soon as possible.

Roles For The Situational Exercise

Mr. Chow (Father). You are the absolute head of the family in
the traditional manner. Although you had little opportunity for
formal education yourself, you are quite happy that your daughter,
Mee Loon, is getting educated. You try to bring up your daughter
according to traditional ways. You have had very little contact with
Bourdin School yourself.

It made you apprehensive to learn that the school was going to
send instead of a teacher, a young man--a student--to teach your
daughter. It also seemed uncomfortable for you that this young man
would be coming to your house for fear of what the neighbors might
make of it.

When the young man arrives, you will be further concerned about
the length of his hair, his clothes, and perhaps his unusual glances.

Mrs. Chow (Mother). You have observed with keen interest the
developments concerning these English lessons since they concern
your daughter. You are a sympathetic person although you are relatively unexposed. Your husband is usually the spokesman for the
family to the outside world and you are therefore not outspoken with

17

important matters. You would, of course, abide by any decision
your husband makes. You are always courteous.

Mee Loon (New Student). You are rather quiet, particularly
in the presence of a teacher or your parents. You have been
having a difficult time with several subjects at Bourdin School, in
large part, because of the need for English lessons. Your English
teacher seems to want you to start taking lessons but you do not feel
strongly one way or the other. You have been brought up to respect
authority.

John (Tutor). You are eager to begin this new project. Besides
the tutoring, you look forward to learning about Chinese culture.
Although you have studied about other foreign societies, you know
little about Chinese customs and traditions. You surmise that
Mee Loon and her parents will welcome you as someone who can introduce her to your country and its customs. You are a good student
and a responsible young person.

Excerpted from: A Manual of Teaching Techniques for Intercultural
Education, University of Massachusetts, Amherst, Mass., 1971.
(with permission)

CHAPTER II

SIMULATIONS

SIMULATION DEVELOPMENT

Robert Alley

Simulation has been defined as an operating model of physical or social situations. To so define it is not to illuminate it very much, however; simulation may be better defined in terms of examples. In the physical sense the drive-o-trainer machines used for teaching safety and driver education to young adults, or the famous Link trainer used in WWII to imitate, or simulate, flying are examples of simulation. More recent years have seen social situations such as ghetto life reproduced in the form of symbolic models for purposes of social simulation as well.

John Gardner once wrote,"All too often we are giving our young people cut flowers when we should be teaching them to grow their own plants." He refers, of course, to the annoying and repetitive habit of educators to "teach about" something rather than to get the students involved in the thought process itself. This module will teach you how to develop your own simulations for your classes.

Simulation may be studied in terms of several factors, some of which are outlined here.

I. Theoretical background

To utilize simulation as a training strategy without a background of knowledge is to be guilty of Silberman's accusation of "mindlessness." It is not adequate to know "about" simulation and to use it just because the trainees like it, which they do. Proper and judicious use of simulation is a must if it is to survive the fad stage and become a permanent part of the training design. To do this a thorough understanding of the training process is necessary as well as an adequate understanding of the theoretical framework underlying simulation.

II. Practical Advantages

Why should the trainer use simulation? What can it bring to the program that the trainer does not already provide in other ways? Some background relative to practical uses of simulation is necessary for the trainer to effectively utilize the strategy in a typical training program.

III. Appropriateness

Simulation is not equally applicable in all disciplines, with all
social or physical situations, or with all people at all times. Knowledge
of its limitations is necessary for effective implementation into training.
Practical models of usage are most valuable in determining appropriateness.

IV. Evaluation

Has the strategy been successful in meeting desired training goals?
No new training strategy should be implemented without adequate evaluation.
In this case, you will have an opportunity to take advantage of the research
done by countless other trainers who have already utilized the concept as
a training strategy.

Each of these factors could be studied as independent topics. However,
it is more likely that they will intermix with one another. Since you will
be studying several sources, it will be most practical to treat each factor
as it emerges rather than trying to separate them out. In the end, the successful development and use of a simulation is the main goal.

DESIGN YOUR OWN SIMULATION

The following pages will guide you step by step through the development
and evaluation of your simulation. In addition you will be given some
criteria for determing appropriateness of use. You may find it useful to
go through the following steps[1] with an existing game before you develop your
own.

STEP ONE: Identify your objectives in teaching this physical or social reali-
           ty in your program. Is it to teach a concept such as values or
perception? Is it to give a "feel" for some realistic situation such as
another culture or an emotionally charged conflict? Or is it to help the
trainee in his decision-making? Be sure to state the goals in terms of
trainee behaviors.

STEP TWO: Select a physical or social reality such as a business management
           problem, a technical development process, an explosive racial
situation, or some reality suitable to your group. Can a model of it be developed? Do so.

STEP THREE: Who are the various principles or actors of the situation? A
             series of persons or teams must be identified. Keep in mind the
number which will demonstrate your model as well as the training needs. Games
often range from two participants to over 30.

---

[1]Adapted from: Foreign Policy Assn. (David King, ed.). SIMULATION
GAMES FOR THE SOCIAL STUDIES CLASSROOM, New York, FPA, 1968, pp. 10-13.

21

STEP FOUR: Create the resources, money, people, etc. that participants
            must have to compete with. Giving precise value to resources
makes participant progress easier to be evaluated. You may wish to make
it a game by setting up precise scoring procedures to determine winners. To
get more ideas review some of the several simulations available. What types
of resources do they utilize?

STEP FIVE: Clearly spell out in writing, or by other means, the objective
            or goal toward which the participant should work in the game.
These may be the welfare of a country, improving one's lot in life, etc.

STEP SIX: Set the necessary limits or rules of behavior. What will be per-
           missible behavior? Keep it consistent with the reality being
modeled. For example, is it realistic to prohibit lying or cheating in a
simulation of a political process? Should there be built-in penalties for
such behavior? Time limits for various steps need to be spelled out too.

STEP SEVEN: Will a "scenario" to set the stage assist the group in getting
             into the model? It is usually a brief discussion of (a) the
history of the situation, (b) the participants, and (c) a description of the
present condition in which participants begin the game.

STEP EIGHT: Plan a de-briefing. This is usually where the trainees learn
             most. What question will you ask trainees?

     The following page presents a model of the steps involved in the pro-
cess of developing a simulation. It will be useful to study it before you
begin.
     Complete the above steps which are outlined on the following pages.
Further directions will follow.

Design Your Own*

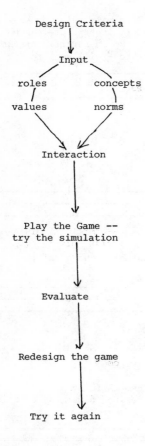

Design Criteria

What do you want to simulate? State goals and objectives.

Input

roles   concepts

values   norms

What is really important to give reality to the simula-tions? What is involved? Persons, ideas, things, processes?

Interaction

What is to be done--by whom-- and when? What are the rules? What are the actions? What happens as consequences of actions?

Play the Game -- try the simulation

Carefully note what happens.

Evaluate

Assess what happens according to the design criteria, input, and interaction.

Redesign the game

Develop new design criteria, applications and interaction. Study the evaluation.

Try it again

*
"Games and Simulation," Wayne County Intermediate School District, Detroit, Michigan. Office of Education--Sponsor Agent. Ed 031 949 (May, 1969).

STEP ONE

List your objectives below. What trainee behaviors will help you know when
they have been reached? It is an excellent idea to incorporate the objectives into the written portions of the simulation so participants know
them as well (use a personalized format such as "you" will be able to....).

_____
_____
_____

STEP TWO

What is your physical or social reality?

_____
_____
_____

Can you model it? Is the model simple, manipulatable, and significant? Coul
the model be sketched here? If so, do so.

_____
_____
_____

STEP THREE

List the principals or teams below. Describe them as fully as needed for
trainee understanding. Think carefully of the desired number of participants to make the model realistic.

_____
_____
_____

STEP FOUR

What resources are the participants to have?

_____
_____
_____

24

Will you try to make it a game? What will be the scoring procedures?
_____
_____
_____

STEP FIVE

What is the objective or goal toward which the participants are to work?
Clearly spell it out here.
_____
_____
_____

STEP SIX

What are the limits of behavior? The rules? Write them out carefully.
Will you need time limits for various parts or steps in the simulation?
_____
_____
_____

STEP SEVEN

Do you need a scenario? Write it below if you feel it is needed.
_____
_____
_____

STEP EIGHT

Plan your debriefing. What questions will you ask participants in order to
tie the activity to valid learning experiences? Prepare your debriefing
below with appropriate questions.
_____
_____
_____

Now your simulation is ready to put together in its general format.
It is a good idea to ask two or more trainers (or better yet-trainees) to

review it and offer suggestions for improvement; better yet try it out or "pilot" it with a small group of trainees. The following questions can be used to guide the review of your simulation.[2] Then when revised use it in your group. Collect evaluative data and revise again.

1. Is the general purpose of the simulation clear? Can the trainees readily determine the objectives?

2. Have you constructed a simplified model? Will the reality simulated by the model be clear to trainees?

3. Are your participants (characters in the simulation) identified clearly? Are they adequately described?

4. Are the resources spelled out? How much money, men, etc. does each participant have? Is the scoring simple and clear if used?

5. Is the goal toward which the participants work clearly designed?

6. Have the limits and rules been defined clearly? Are the stages (rounds) of play spelled out?

7. Have you written a scenario? Do your participants know the conditions under which they begin?

8. How will you debrief the participants? Have you written down some questions for them to consider? Would it be helpful to let them in on such questions in advance?

Now, put it together in final form and give it a try.

---

[2]Adapted from: FPA _ibid_.

CULTURE SIMULATION AS A TRAINING TOOL

Melvin Schnapper

    The lengthy record of failures compiled by all aid-giving nations
points to a lack of cross-cultural knowledge and understanding among
the planners and executors of international development projects.
In spite of this lack, the issue of appropriate intercultural communication adaptation training has not been effectively handled by
either private firms or government agencies. By intercultural training,
I mean sequences of activities--exercise, lectures, readings, discus-
sions--that focus on cultural differences. These differences may be
the values, goals, attitudes, behaviors, or assumptions that characterize different cultural and social groups. The training process should
force trainees to consider these differences and the effects they might
have on the trainees' work in other cultures.
    Although intercultural preparation of this kind is generally
recognized to be of great importance, few persons know how to do it
effectively. Some even claim it cannot be done. Thus, many international development experts who go overseas either have had no training
at all or have had a hurried briefing, consisting, at worst, of
discussions with embassy officials or agency personnel or, at best, of
two to three weeks of lectures.
    This article will describe the approach taken by the Canadian
International Development Agency (CIDA) in providing sound preparation for its international operations personnel.
    During April-July 1971, I served as a consultant to the CIDA
Briefing Centre. My function was to integrate all of their
concerns; to make knowledge and experience complementary instead of
conflicting; sequenced instead of fragmented; real, felt, and personal
instead of unreal, removed, and abstract. The other members of the
team were an applied anthropologist, a geographer/linguist, an area
studies coordinator, and a Briefing Centre coordinator. My wife was
the family relations counselor on the team.

    The Program Design. The product of our interaction was an inten-
sive "survival" simulation exercise (see below for the scenarios
which took the first seven days of the program, followed by three days

of a more traditional but self-directed area studies program. The
first part of the program was intended to give interculturally naive
participants an intercultural experience that would make them more
aware of their own "Canadianness" and an opportunity to gain new perceptions and practice new behaviors. We also wanted to provide an
experience during the first phase of the program that would enable
participants to ask more sophisticated questions during the second
phase. During the second phase they would have access to various
sources of information--people who had been abroad, host nationals,
area experts, film, and a resource library.

To promote a desirable learning environment for the simulation,
the large number of participants (140) was divided into smaller groups
of twelve to fifteen each. The group format was used to facilitate
involvement, increase psychological comfort, promote interpersonal
sharing, and to enable persons to practice their intercultural communication skills. Unlike many other pre-departure programs, we
saw the whole family as the basic unit to be trained, not only the
working spouse; therefore, wives as well as some dozen teenagers
also participated. Husbands and wives were not in the same group as
their spouses however.

The groups were led by a staff composed of former international
volunteers (Canadian University Service Overseas, British Graduate
Volunteer Service Overseas, U.S. Peace Corps) or persons working with
Indian and Eskimo groups in Canada. One trainer was Jamaican and
another Canadian Indian. Thus, the staff itself presented a model
of international and intercultural cooperation to the trainees.

Each group was asked to simulate a situation in which it has
crash-landed in one of four environments--desert, mountain, swamp,
or island. The members of the group then had to evolve a way of coping
with the environment and each other. They identified each member's
skills, divided up labor, defined roles and dealt with the issues of
religion, parenthood, family structure, sexuality, education, etc.
In short, they evolved a new culture to cope with a new situation and
a new environment.

New Cultures. The groups went about this in unique and creative
ways. Some dismissed the nuclear family or rigid sexual roles. Some
abolished any kind of formal education, choosing instead informal ways
of educating their offspring. All the groups examined their Canadian
culture, retaining what they admired and discarding what they did
not like. During this process they learned that there were more ways
to cope with survival than they had been exposed to. They also dis-
covered how culture serves as an adaptive mechanism for different
groups in different circumstances. The training program ensured that
the participants would experience concretely these more abstract but
necessary concepts, which would help them to appreciate other cultures
and to work more effectively overseas.

One of the peak learning experiences came when, four days into the simulation, each group was brought into contact with another group. They were then separated to do a cross-cultural ("we" and "they") analysis and then brought back together to present their analyses to each other. In every case, one group felt superior to the other group! No matter how different the cultures were from each other, or from Canadian society, each group felt that it had used the previous days in the most productive way, had evolved a more functional culture, and had chosen most wisely what to preserve and what to discard.

Most participants were shocked at their own reactions. They felt, and later came to appreciate, that strong feelings of ethnocentricity could be formed in three days. The lesson was emphasized by the fact that these feelings were about another group of Canadians (even a group with their own spouses in it)! "If I feel this way about my fellow Canadians, how will I feel about the host nationals where the differences are so much more vast?"asked many of the participants. At this point they were more than ready, even eager, to discuss concepts like cultural identity and intercultural perception.

"Experts". Another very significant encounter occurred on the fifth day. Groups from different environments were asked to prepare international development aid "experts." These experts found that the experience of their own "donor" group had conditioned them to make invalid assumptions about the "recipient" group and hence had a negative effect in their helping efforts. These assumptions were based upon the very different experiences, values, socio-cultural institutions, goals, etc., which they carried from their old group into the new. Most confusing of all to the "experts" was that the groups they had come to help often decided that they either did not want help, wanted a different kind of help, or simply resented the way in which the help was offered. Very often the "experts" sought to convince the recipient group of the benefits that would accrue if such assistance was accepted. Most "experts" tried more to convince than to listen to the real needs of the recipients.

When the "experts" returned to their groups, they helped "train" a second pair of consultants, who in turn went to the recipient group. The second pair fared a little better, but were often hampered by the inaccurate perceptions of the first pair. In this sequence of experiences, most participants learned about change agentry and the need for listening with skepticism to those "who have been there."

At the end of the experiential simulation, participants were regrouped according to the area or country they were going to. They were presented with a list of persons, films, books, and slides which they could pursue during the last three days. With the simulation fresh in their minds, most groups structured themselves into ten-hour working days. They were eager to acquire the information that related both to their recent experience and to their anticipated experience overseas.

The participants and staff felt that the questions that were asked were far superior to those of previous groups, who had under-

gone more traditional programs. Equally important was the fact
that the interest of the participants shifted noticeably from purely
technical and logistical matters to concerns about intercultural and
interpersonal adjustment problems. A new realism emerged about the
difficulties of successful adaptation; many realized that technical
and administrative competency in one's culture does not guarantee
success in a different culture.

All who were involved in the program considered it a great success.
The participants thoroughly enjoyed it. Even the thirty or so CIDA's
who had been abroad before realized how much they had missed during
their previous tour as a result of not having had this kind of preparation. It should be noted that, in addition to the intercultural
training, all contractual, logistic, administrative, and medical
procedures were taken care of during the program.

   Conclusions. The program described could have a general application for private companies or government agencies sending persons
abroad for international operations. Several aspects of the program
lead to this conclusion: 1) generalized concepts important for
intercultural effectiveness can be experienced by the participant in
the training situation; 2) specific techniques within the general
approach described can be tailored to the specific job, cultural context, skills and ambitions of the training staff; and 3) this experiential, participant-involving approach is far superior to conventional
approaches that are exclusively information-centered. Experiential
training gives participants "learning how to learn" tools that will
enable them to continue learning and sharpening their intercultural
skills once in the actual situation.

   Survival Exercise: "Desert" Scenario. The chartered aircraft
in which you are flying to your assignment overseas develops engine
trouble and has to crash land. Nobody is hurt, but you have just time
to grab your hand luggage and get out before the plane bursts into
flames. There is no chance of rescue and the area in which you find
yourself is uninhabited.

As the sun rises,a barren scene unfolds as a backdrop to the charred
shell of the chartered aircraft. The night air, which has been amazingly
cold, slowly warms,and the desert haze burns off to reveal an uninter-
rupted treeless horizon that offers no visible sign of shade or moisture.
Dry grasses growing in intermittent tufts are widely interspersed with
small, thick-leaved plants and dead flowers that must have bloomed
during more succulent times. The heat becomes more intense as the day
progresses, and a pressing need for water is realized in an area where
only dry stream beds with cracked and hardened bottoms are to be found.
Periodically gigantic boulders thrust skyward and at their shaded bases,
sheltered from the hot wind, grows greener vegetation. Small patches
of dark moister-looking soil are also found in this vicinity. The whole
land is of a reddish hue and is very rocky in places as if at some time
volcanic activity had occurred. In many places it is scarred with deep
gullies torn out by infrequent, torrential rainstorms. Much rock of a
porous, rough nature is strewn about in these gullies. In the shaded

areas are found many small holes which contain evidence of habitation
by both herbivorous and carnivorous animals. Beyond this total monotony
of heat-ridden, undulating redness lies only a repetition of the same
from horizon to horizon.

Survival Exercise: "Swamp" Scenario. The chartered aircraft
in which you are flying to your assignment overseas develops engine
trouble and has to crash land. Nobody is hurt, but you have just
time to grab your hand luggage and get out before the plane bursts
into flames. There is no chance of rescue and the area in which you
find yourself is uninhabited.

The breakers pulverize the stricken aircraft as the incoming tide
covers the mudflat where the forced landing was made. Beyond the reach
of the waves, stretch the reeds and grasses of a bog. As the land
rises, the bog turns to meadow and at the summit of the hill rise a few
tortured, flat-topped trees. The island is low and wind-swept as is
evidenced by the dunes above the swamp. As the elevation increases,
sea cliffs rise until the island falls abruptly to the sea. No natural
source of fresh water is visible. Animal life consists mainly of birds
and smaller mammals, including rabbits and mice. In addition, signs
of wild goats are seen. In the shallower waters where the wrecked
plane lies, there are shellfish and small sharks which make wading
hazardous. Below the cliffs the waves are broken by smashed rock and
debris which tell of severe battering by both wind and waves. The
air is warm and very dry, telling of a long period of drought,as does
the brownness of the grass and trees on the hillside. Rainless clouds
scud across the horizon which is completely flat, bearing signs of
neither land nor life.

Survival Exercise: "Mountain" Scenario. The chartered aircraft
in which you are flying to your assignment overseas develops engine
trouble and has to crash land. Nobody is hurt, but you have just time
to grab your hand luggage and get out before the plane bursts into flames.
There is no chance of rescue and the area in which you find yourself
is uninhabited.

The wind screams about the wreckage of the aircraft and from the
sheltered leeward side unfolds a stark, unfriendly scene. High cliffs
rise out of wind-swept alpine meadows where patches of snow remain,
greyed by fast-blown grit. The wind eternally tears at the mountain,
threatening to topple any precariously upright creature into one of the
many ravines. Flattened against the ground grows a hardy type of grass
that is in many places decorated with small delicate flowers. Stunted
bushes covered with fruit cling to the ground in the shelter of the
cliffs. On all sides, snow-capped peaks pierce the grey layers of
clouds and rear upwards into the blue sky. One cannot see below the
clouds,and even if that were possible, the vastness and the emptiness
would only be magnified. The thin air makes prolonged effort difficult,
especially when the wind snatches away what little breath there is to
be drawn. On closer inspection, a small rodent-like animal is seen
scurrying into a cleft in the rock. A shadow passes over the ground
and draws attention to the sky where two eagles circle in search of
prey. A break in the protective layer of cloud below reveals sheer
cliffs dropping to rolling elevations and more steep meadows that
are speared by sharp pinnacles of jagged rock. The clouds close,and
as companions only the wind, the peaks and the sky remain.

31

Survival Exercise: "Lush Island" Scenario. The chartered
aircraft in which you are flying to your assignment overseas develops engine trouble and has to crash land. Nobody is hurt, but you
have just time to grab your hand luggage and get out before the plane
bursts into flames. There is no chance of rescue and the area in which
you find yourself is uninhabited.

From the wreckage at the summit of the hill, all that is visible
is a sea of waving treetops, occasionally punctuated by a change of
colour or of height. The land slopes steeply to the east where it
disappears unaltered except for the occasional glimmer from a distant,
nameless river. The sloping floor of the forest is covered with dense
underbrush which is intertwined with fast-growing vines and creepers.
Wet, trailing mosses hang from the branches of the trees and thick
lichens and fungi flourish on the trunks. Little sunlight penetrates
below the underbrush which is sufficiently dense to impair rapid movement. This thick growth provides shelter for many kinds of birds
as is evidenced by the preponderance of noise. The pronounced slope
of the land, combined with high humidity and heavy rainfall, has
caused considerable dissection by streams. On the edges of the banks
sunlight penetrates, and fruit-bearing bushes sometimes grow. Where the
slope falls away quickly, there are rockfalls which have resisted
jungle encroachment apart from small bushes and mosses. Here the sun
shines and small reptiles are visible on the rocks. Everywhere is the
inescapable hum of the insect population which defies even the most
diligent swatter. The air is very moist and heavy, yet the clouds
promise more rain in the afternoon. Farther down where the slope is
less pronounced, the undergrowth thins until only a canopy of broadleafed
trees shuts out the sunlight and leaves the ground shrouded in mist
and darkness.

USING BAFA BAFA*

Ann Gillespie

Description

Participants are divided into two groups, Alpha culture and Beta culture. Each group is taught a fictitious set of cultural values, behaviors and communication styles. The game is especially designed to simulate two quite different cultures, and then to involve participants in cultural exchange, with all its attendant problems of culture shock, adaptation to a strange environment, return to the home culture and the like. The participants are urged to "get into the spirit" of the game, to exaggerate, and to have fun acting out the designated roles for the duration of the game. It is designed to cause people to stereotype and misperceive each other, to make wrong assumptions about the other culture, and to develop a quickly internalized set of in-group behaviors and attitudes toward out-groups.

Goals

(a) To increase awareness of our own cultural identity and that of the culturally different; to increase intercultural communication skills; to increase understanding of "culture" and its function in interpersonal relations; to understand the problems of adapting in a new environment; to become better interpreters of nonverbal communication; and to stimulate thoughtful discussion about differences in values, attitudes, and communication styles across cultures.

(b) To have fun and get to know each other, to practice new roles and express oneself in a non-threatening situation, to become aware of the effects of social interaction and dynamics of groups, extracting from the simulated experience examples of incidents which remind participants of real-life happenings thereby personalizing the game.

Strengths

Its ability to draw people into the game emotionally, so that they learn the principles of intercultural communication through direct involvement rather than through the presentation of abstract concepts. Sharpens communication skills so people become effective in future intercultural encounters. It's fun!

Weaknesses

The trainer must be wary of taking too long for explanations. It takes skill to coach people, get their energy up, be lively and enthusiastic in both presentation and direction of the game. Don't take this game too seriously! Another weakness is the simplicity of the two social systems. Participants may be bothered by the rigidity of

33

of the rules and the lack of identification of Alpha and Beta to any
cultures they know. It must be explained that it is the process of
intercultural relations that the game presents, more than the actual,
real-life content of a culture.

Pitfalls

This is a powerful exercise and there is some chance that people
will be left with unresolved feelings after the game. Trainers must
be ready to deal with some strong reactions. Be sure to take time for
working out these feelings and resolving conflicts. The game should
be conducted early in the day so that there is plenty of time for processing and people are not tired.

Leadership

Two trainers are needed, one for each cultural group. They
should be experienced and able to deal with the variety of reactions
that can occur in this game. They must be enthusiastic, able to keep
others going when their interest flags and have stamina.

Processing

At least an hour should be set aside for discussion, follow-up on
themes and small groups. People should be encouraged to explore their
feelings about the experience and give one another feedback about their
reactions. The leader brings the real issues into the consciousness
of the group and encourages sharing between participants.

Themes or Topics for Discussion

Male-female relationships (cross-culturally or in one culture)
Family life--norms, beliefs, communication
Work and play in cultures
Self-esteem and adaptation in new environments
Readiness for study abroad--orientation
Readiness for study in the U.S.--Foreign Student orientation
Community programs--how awareness of the components in inter-
    cultural communication can enhance them
Interrelationship of language and culture
Materialism, competition, alienation
Friendship, hospitality, intimacy
Task orientation vs. relationship orientation

Equipment

A set of materials and a trainer's manual. The set costs $23.00
and can be ordered from Simile II.

Group Size

Between twelve and forty participants.

---

*Simulation Game by Gary Shirts. Published by Simile II, 1150
Silverado, La Jolla, California 92037.

AID TO MINORIANS

Robert Kohls, Tad Edlich,
Margo Kiely and Bill Hoffman

I had often used roleplay as a training technique in Peace
Corps training programs, but the Live-In Debriefing Workshop for
a Peace Corps training program for Tunisia was my first attempt
to engage the entire body of trainees (27 at the Workshop) in a
single roleplay activity. The traditional roleplay setting usually
engages a single trainee with a single American or host country
national staff member playing the role of an official or some
such similar professional, in his home country. In my past experience I had, on one or two occasions, engaged four people
(including two trainees) in a roleplay scene. Any learning which
the entire training body received from such limited participation
had to come, for most of them, from their role as observers instead
of active participants.

The "Aid to Minorians" roleplay situation (scenarios follow)
was, in my estimation, extremely successful. It involved everyone completely. The scene developed not into a single-focus,
unified setting, but as might be expected, into a chaotic multi-
faceted "happening." But at no point did it get out of control.
There were times when there were alternately, one, two, or three
centers of activity going simultaneously, with the fluidity to
move from several centers back to one or two again.

The game was designed to make the participants aware of the
helper-helpee relationship. The Minorians wore black crepe paper
armbands, the Majorian, white. The Minorians had only the barest
supplies to work with - newsprint, brass fasteners, and string -
while the Majorians arrived laden down with luxurious goodies -
colored crepe paper, colored tissue paper, paper doilies, scotch
tape, masking tape, and scissors (representing their technical
superiority and affluence).

The discussion which followed indicated many of the trainees
came away from the simulation with insightful understandings of
such things as how it feels to try to help and be rejected, to
want to "go it alone" with your own limited supplies, to fear
that acceptance of aid will lead, eventually, to domination and
curtailment of freedom, etc.,etc..

The discussion eventually culminated in a frank look at how
it might feel to be the Tunisian recipient of help from an American
PCV, given Tunisia's long history of political domination and her
newly-gained independence and national pride. The realization that
what arrangements and agreements have been accomplished for them

35

to serve as PCU's in Tunisia have been made by ministries and officials, and how it might feel to accept help from a youthful representative of the wealthiest "Majoria" in the world were all sobering insights.

Instruction to Minorians

You are residents of the country of Minoria. Minoria is not a new country but a very old one with a noble history and a rich culture. Unfortunately, your country has been dominated by other nations for so long that you are just now beginning to regain a sense of independence and pride. You have finally been able to shake yourself free of those countries which had dominated you and exploited you for so long, and you have a great jealousy of your hard-won freedom to run your own country the way you want to.

Unfortunately, one of the problems that besets you is the fact that you have few natural resources, and because you have been dominated by others for so long, you have not been able to develop the ones you have nor the technology to make use of them. Poverty is a problem in your country, but it is one you have learned to live with and even to accept as the normal way of life.

This is the anniversary of your independence, and you are searching for some appropriate focus around which the new national pride can develop: perhaps a monument, symbol, or something similar. Your task is to begin discussing what kind of project will best symbolize that pride and then to construct it with the materials and resources you have at hand. You want (partly out of pride) to use your own native materials to the extent possible, but also because you do not have the money to import materials, and, too, because you do not want to become indebted to outsiders. You are especially wary of gifts with political strings attached.

You have just received word from the Ministry that in the next twenty minutes a team of people will be arriving from a country called Majoria. Although you have never had an opportunity to meet any Majorians, Majoria is well known to you, since it is one of the leading countries in the world. Its resources seem to be endless. While you are pleased for suggestions and appreciative of help, you resist any type of patronizing and are anxious to do your own thing. Other nations have dominated you for centuries and you are suspicious of Trojan horses.

After twenty minutes of planning, you will have no more than thirty minutes to execute the plans you have made. On with your monument! Long live Minoria!

Instructions to Majorians

You are the fortunate citizens of Majoria. Majoria's technology, natural resources, and wealth make it a country without peers in the modern world. Your people have solved the scourges of earlier centuries: epidemics, hunger, limited production, illiteracy, etc.. People in your country worry little about survival, and more about opportunity in a land of abundance.

Unfortunately, there are other countries that are far less fortunate. Many people in your country are concerned about their plight - some out of guilt of having so much while others have so little; others out of the realism that the world will not long be safe if the imbalance of technology, resources, and materials continues; some out of need to find new markets for their own products, which will help the developing nations as well as your own

country. Because of your genuine concern for less fortunate people
and your idealism, you have volunteered to go to an obscure little
country named Minoria.

Minoria is a poor underdeveloped nation. Side by side there
are the contrasts: affluence and want, the handsomely dressed
leaders and the starving beggars, new buildings and shacks without
sanitation, the bespectacled professor and the illiterate country
people. Behind the plush front, the statistics of hunger, disease,
and unemployment tell the real story. Minoria is new among the
nations of the world, and its leaders, policy-makers, and technicians
are inexperienced at their work. Frequently, things seem to be done
on the merest whim and have little relation to the country's basic
needs.

Minoria needs many things. It is struggling to survive in
the modern world. Many fear it will not. Its primary need is firm
insistence on an ordering of priorities to place the few resources
where the greatest need is. Second, the country needs other resources
to supplement its own. Third, they need technical assistance and
foreign investments to make sure what they construct endures and
what they have will be used well.

You have ten minutes to plan what you will do to help before
arriving in that country. After your arrival, you will be expected
to help the Minorians plan a major project that will benefit their
country, and to help execute that plan using the materials you have
at hand.

Remember, you will be evaluated on your ability to:
1.   help them reset priorities which match their needs;
2.   help them use the materials you have brought wisely;
3.   make helpful construction hints and give technical aid on
      the project that is finally decided upon.

THE EAST-WEST GAME

(Emperor's Pot)

Experiment in International Living

        This is a simulation for 15 to 40 people and takes 1-1/2 to 2 hours.
Leave ample time for processing. PHASE I: The participants are divided
into two groups, East and West, and brought together separately in two
different rooms with a trainer to develop their cultures and strategies.
PHASE II: A delegation from the West visits the East while simultaneously
a delegate from the East visits the West. PHASE III: East and West get
together in own groups to assess what happened. PHASE IV: Trainers process
the experience. The game has been called "The Emperor's Pot" because the
treasured artifact has sometimes been identified as a sacred pot.

                                    EAST

Instructions:

        Your group represents an ancient Eastern culture. You are poor but
proud.
        A highly treasured artifact is in your possession. It dates back
to 400 A.D. It is a national treasure, in fact the national treasure, and
culturally you cannot give it up under any circumstances. The other side
(West) wants it. Their delegation is under strong pressure from the West
to return with the artifact. (You may wish to identify one key behavior
which, if demonstrated by the West, will win them the treasure.)
        However, it is in the nature of your culture to be very agreeable,
to be very polite, to try always to answer affirmatively, whether you mean
it or not. You never come out directly with a flat negative in the negotiations. You never tell their delegates that they will never get the artifact. You dissemble if necessary; you seem to agree or go along, because
culturally you never wish to offend.
        Culturally, it is important for you to avoid strong, direct eye con-
tact with the delegates or visitors from the West. You look them in the
eye, but never in a fixed, hard, direct look of any duration.
        Typically, even your negotiating team (your delegates to the West)
will practice the ancient art of dealing through a third party. Example:
one of you has the role of Chief Spokesman (a senior scholar and official),
who may act as one of your delegates to the West, or may negotiate at home
with the delegates from the West. And while he will do some of the talking in either situation, he will defer often to one of the other members of
your group and let that other person carry on some if not most of the conversation with the other side. The West will not understand what dynamic

                                     38

is operating here, but that is their problem.

Situational note: The West will be sending delegates to your culture to try to find a way to persuade you to relinquish the national treasure. You will observe their style and make notes on your assumptions, based on the way they behave and talk in your culture during the Phase II negotiations. At the same time (Phase II) a delegation of your people will go to the West (to their Embassy let's assume) where their officials will try to persuade some of your people on their home ground.

Your list of cultural values is attached. There will be a staff person in your room to help with questions during the Phase I planning period. During that time you will sort out your various roles, decide who should go to the West, who and how many, and who should remain in the East to negotiate with the West delegates. You should also decide upon the approach you will take in Phase II.

Roles:

Chief Spokesman
Minister of Education and Culture
Security Officer
Political Officer
Protocol Officer
Information Officer
Recorder--to list all the assumptions, values, etc., of other side
Astrologer/Time-keeper--to keep each phase exactly on schedule
GOD (Group Organizational Director)--the overall organizer of East Team
Advisors--all others
Most Honored Grandmother
Spokesman #2 (most honored)

EAST--CULTURAL TRAITS

(these are the items governing your behavior)

"WE"--Performance is conditioned by role in society, as opposed to individualism.

OVERLAPPING EGO--Expectations/morality of community more important than those of individual. Individual always in social role. Cannot do anything to conflict with group.

FORM--Outward form is of major importance. Manners extremely important, must participate in activities considered important by group, even though one disagrees.

PASSIVISM--Confucian idea of endurance is prevalent. Acceptance of fate, life, etc.

PRAGMATISM--Confucian or community morality is applied to social issues and problems.

PROGRESS--Change is both negative and positive. Technical change necessary; social change bad.

NATURE--Nature is considered beautiful/good. Conformity to rule of nature considered good.

EFFICIENCY--Considered less important than higher values such as form, face, conformity to custom.

TIME--Not precisely measured, except in business/science. Time not a primary consideration. The present, not the future, is given utmost

        consideration.
HISTORY--History is seen as a cyclical phenomenon rather than a linear
        progression.
HUMILITY--Humility is related to social status. One never takes advantage
        of one's rank. One must always defer to one of higher social rank,
        must always try to appear humble. Persons of higher rank must
        even make attempts to defer to and honor special inferiors.
DISCIPLINE--Pre-school = much freedom, little discipline. School age = dis-
        cipline begins at home and from teachers in school. Considered a
        function of the school system at this age rather than a function of
        the parents. Adulthood = many responsibilities to family and com-
        munity. Old age = great freedom, shown much respect, considered
        to have great wisdom.
MOBILITY--Important because one has duties to family and community.
WORK--A means to an end rather than an end in itself. Has no value in
        itself.
MONEY--Saving for the sake of saving is seldom considered a virtue. Some
        attitudes towards money involve concepts of "face"--i.e., spending
        an entire year's income for elaborate ceremonies, wedding, etc., to
        increase or maintain family prestige. Price is regarded as an in-
        dex of quality.
AGE--Great reverence for age, which means wisdom, authority, great per-
        spective on life. Age brings certain privileges (a girl is not a
        woman until married and a mother). One always uses honorific terms
        when addressing an elder.
EDUCATION--A discipline, and a reflection on family prestige. Means of
        raising whole family status. Confucian idea of education to create
        the true gentleman.
AUTHORITY--Confucian values stress the cautions. Obedience to authority.
        Individual rights bear little consideration. Vertically organized
        hierarchy regarded as most orderly and harmonious.
MORAL SUPERIORITY--A moral smugness stemming from a conviction that EAST's
        people are a special people with a set of values and conditions that
        made them unique.

                                  WEST

Instructions:

        Your group represents an authentic Western culture. You are rich
and powerful.
        A highly treasured artifact is in the possession of the East. It
is a most valuable part of their ancient cultural heritage, and although
they are a poor country, they will be reluctant to give it up. However,
you have been assigned the task by your national museum with strong urging
from the Government itself, to obtain this national treasure for your
country's own collection. Money is no problem.
        Thus your task is to assemble a delegation, send them to the East
(you decide who goes, how many, what approach they should use...as long
as the approach appears to you to be compatible with the cultural values
listed on the next page). In plainest terms, your group has been sent to
the East to bring back the artifact at whatever cost, although you cannot

come right out and say this during negotiations with the East. They are
known in the world as shrewd traders, even though they are relatively
poor, but you have been instructed to operate on the supposition that every
man has his price.
        Culturally, it is important for you and your negotiators to figure
out which approaches are acceptable to the other side, in order to smooth
out the path to your objective, which is the artifact, but at the same time
you should try to stay within the value system defined for you in the next
pages.
        Typically, you tend to be success-oriented, hard-working, efficient;
you plan ahead and try to use time productively.
        Situational note: When told, you will send your delegation to the
East. While they are negotiating, this team will also be recording observations about the ways in which the Easterners operate, and making assumptions about them. At the same time, a delegation from the East will come
to the West (let's assume the meeting takes place in your Embassy in their
country) during which period you will try to persuade their delegates about
the merits of your case...for the artifact, simultaneously trying to find
out from them what their price might be, etc.
        Your list of cultural values is attached. There will be a staff
person in your room to help with questions during the Phase I planning
period. During that time you will sort out, you will consult the value
list, decide who and how many should go to the East to negotiate, and who
and how many should remain in the West to negotiate with their delegation.
        Roles:
Curator of National Museum (expert on Oriental Art)
Diplomatic Officer
Public Relations man or woman
CIA agent posing as an Area Studies Specialist
Journalist
Chief of your task-group (forceful administrator)
Recorder--to list all assumptions, values, etc., of other side
Time-keeper--to keep each phase of exercise exactly on schedule
GOD (Group Organizational Director)--the overall organizer of the West team
Advisor--all others

                    WEST--CULTURAL TRAITS
            (these are the items governing your role behavior)

"I"--Ego-centrism
INDIVIDUALISM--Self-reliance, initiative expected from each. Status
        achieved by own efforts. Economic, social, political equal oppor-
        tunity regarded as right of individual. Achievement is good, and
        requires competitiveness. Competition expected.
SOCIAL CONFORMITY--Outward conformity to opinions of others and to dress
        has certain value in society.
ACTIVISM--Being active, especially in face of uncertainty, is a virtue.
        Achievement and goal-oriented activities are strongly stressed.
PRAGMATISM--Practical ingenuity applied to social as well as materialis-
        tic problems.
PROGRESS--Change in itself is good. Improvement, especially personal, is
        a duty. Man is supposed to work in order to control nature.

                              41

EFFICIENCY--Applies not only to machines but to social organizations and
        personalities.
TIME--Precisely measured and must be used productively and efficiently.
HISTORY--Seen as a linear progression.
AGGRESSIVENESS--Ambition, competition, self-assertiveness to achieve suc-
        cess are emphasized. High status, once attained, does not confer
        right to treat lower class as "inferior." Personal excelling is
        good, but empty boasts, or boasting about success are bad.
DISCIPLINE--Pre-school = discipline from parents. School age = increased
        freedom and responsibility. Adulthood = time of greatest freedom.
        Old age considered less productive, less active, an epoch of in-
        capability, less freedom.
MOBILITY--Great physical and social mobility seen as good.
WORK--Valued as an end in itself. Personal effort, energy output = good.
        Laziness = bad.
MONEY--An economic tool, plus yardstick for social status, influence,
        power, satisfaction.
YOUTH--Highly valued. Old people wish they were young again. Elders feel
        outmoded by rapid change.
EDUCATION--Means to an end. Reflection on family prestige. Means to attain
        skill, money, status.
AUTHORITY--Rules/laws generally obeyed, but don't like to be ordered to obey.
        Authorities must not infringe upon individual rights. Mild suspicion
        of authority.
MORAL SUPERIORITY--A moral smugness stemming from convictions that WEST's
        people are a special people with a set of values and conditions that
        have made them unique.

Prepared with the assistance of Toby S. Frank and Shiela Ramsey.

CHAPTER III

<u>THE CONTRAST-AMERICAN</u>

SIMULATING INTERCULTURAL COMMUNICATION

THROUGH ROLE-PLAYING*

Edward C. Stewart, Jack Danielson and Robert J. Foster

Nature of the Simulation Exercises

The model used in the simulation exercises is different in several respects from those usually identified with simulation. This model is essentially social-psychological in character, in that an attempt has been made to represent perceptual and experiential reality (including the unconscious aspect of experience) rather than to reproduce, point for point, physical or environmental variables.

The primary building blocks and systematic dimensions of a social-psychological model are cognitive variables--in this instance, cultural values and assumptions. Representation of physical and environmental aspects is important only to the extent that the training exercise must be plausible--it must look and feel like a "real life" situation to the trainee.

Furthermore, it is not necessary for the cognitive variables themselves to be a faithful reproduction of an actual culture. In these exercises, a synthetic but plausible culture was created to contrast with American values and assumptions, for use in guiding the behavior of the "foreigner" in the role-playing exercise. The essential feature of the exercises is a representation of the social-psychological aspects of interaction between people who hold differing values and assumptions; the key function of the exercises is to induce a cognitive confrontation, with accompanying emotional investment and behavioral confrontation.

In this sense the simulation model can be referred to as "functional," since the focus is on process and conditions important to training, rather than on faithful reproduction of the content of the cognitive underpinning of any particular culture. However, American values and assumptions must be accurately depicted, because it is insight into one's own values and assumptions that permits the growth of a perspective which recognizes that differing sets of values and assumptions exist (i.e., cultural relativism), and development of the potential for greater understanding of another culture.

_____

*Human Relations Research Organization, Alexandria, Va., 1969. (Materials included here are excerpts from a longer article.)

44

A confrontation during cultural interaction must be distinguished from competition between participants for available rewards. Cognitive confrontation, as the term is used here, involves a dissonance or incongruity between ways of thinking and perceiving, rather than concern over who will win. Rivalry may occur during interaction, but it would be derived from a conflict in cultural perspectives rather than from a conflict of interests as such.

In the simulation exercises, the cognitive confrontation is embedded in experience-based training using role-playing to achieve the requirement that the student be effectively involved in learning. This training approach engages the trainee behaviorally and emotionally while simultaneously exposing him to cultural values and assumptions different from his own.

The contrast he encounters in the exercises provides the trainee with a situation that stimulates the dynamic processes of "unfreezing," "moving," and "refreezing" that constitute cognitive-affective learning. Emotionally and behaviorally involved in the role-playing situation, the trainee is "unfrozen" from his habitual modes of perception by the experience of being exposed to the consequences of acting upon his own cultural-cognitive frame of reference. The unfreezing is facilitated by exposure to new views which, while inconsistent with the trainee's own views, are presented in a way that makes them difficult to refute; the trainee finds that what seemed to be "normal" (American) solutions to the task at hand are not readily understood or accepted by the "foreigner."

In the unfreezing process the two sets of cultural values (American and Contrast-American) serve as mirrors for each other so as to increase the level of cultural awareness of oneself and of the "foreign" other. The cognitive confrontation brings one's own values and assumptions into question, making the trainee more aware of the cultural determinant in himself. Self-awareness, in turn, results in greater understanding and empathy with the values and assumptions of a member of another culture; continuing the reciprocal relationship, this increased understanding once again yields a deeper cultural self-awareness which increases other-awareness ad infinitum. Once unfrozen, the trainee is in a semifluid state concerning his own culturally derived perceptions and begins to evaluate the Contrast-American's values and assumptions more freely (relativistically).

Under optimal training circumstances, the trainee would here begin to forge bridges between his cultural position and that of his counterpart, gradually evolving a mutually compatible position. Cultural empathy and suspension of the moral judgments emanating from his own culture are necessary to sustain and nourish the growth of such an emerging position. This process constitutes the "moving" portion of the learning cycle. The actual creation and maintenance of such a position then signifies the desired refreezing at a new level of awareness and behavior.

In broader perspective, the unfreezing process simply sets the stage for future learning ("learning how to learn"), with the payoffs coming in increments each time the person faces new experiences at home or abroad. It is the latter type of continuous relearning that is the primary objective of most cognitive-affective training efforts of this sort.

The learning process does not involve sacrifice of either the trainee's personal values or his advisory mission. On the contrary, by becoming aware of possible alternative cultural positions, he should become _more_ aware of his own cultural values (and blinders) and _increase_ his flexibility in the kinds of approaches or avenues he can utilize.

Development of the Intercultural Simulation Exercises

The paradigm used in the development of the simulation exercises calls for at least one American participant (advisor) and his foreign counterpart to meet in an intercultural encounter. The American advisor role is played spontaneously by a trainee on the basis of background and scene information that is provided him. While this role is indirectly controlled by means of the "scenes" (defined below), the role of the counterpart (hereafter often referred to as the auxiliary) is directly and deliberately manipulated according to specified values and assumptions that are to determine his reactions to the American trainee. The steps by which the simulation was constructed are as follows:

(1) The literature describing American cultural patterns was reviewed and analyzed in terms of the problems American officials typically encounter overseas. The modal (middle class) values and assumptions were codified along dimensions judged relevant to overseas performance according to a modification of a schema suggested by Kluckhohn and Strodtbeck (1).

(2) Contrasting dimensions were defined to yield artificial opposite-to-American cultural values and assumptions ("Contrast-American culture").

(3) A series of plausible overseas advisory situations ("scenes") were developed to elicit culturally determined behavior from an American trainee.

(4) Role-playing auxiliaries were trained to reflect the Contrast-American values and assumptions in a way which would bring about strong involvement of the American trainee.

(5) Role-playing confrontations were played out and formats for feedback to the trainee explored.

These five stages define the major components in the design and development of the training and are treated in more detail later.

For purposes of analysis, culture may be examined at four levels: concrete behavior, values, assumptions, and generalized cultural forms. The last three are necessarily derived from observations of behavior, but can be usefully treated as a motivational explanation underlying most human behavior. Viewed at the individual level they are, in effect, internalized components of personality that are generally shared with other members of the cultural group.

"Values" are relatively concrete, discrete, and specific; for instance, typical American values are the sanctity of private property, the desirability of physical comfort, and the need for tangible measures of success. Values also have a quality of "oughtness" and are relatively available to individual awareness (C. Kluckhohn, 8). A person will often discuss values when explaining his own or others' feel-

46

ings or behavior.

"Assumptions," on the other hand, are more abstract and more out-side of conscious awareness. They represent the predispositions the individual employs to pattern the world, and are usually felt by the individual to be an aspect of the world itself and not simply his per-ception of it. Examples of American assumptions are a predisposition to see the self as separate from the world, and the usual endorsement of "doing" as the preferred means of self-expression. (1)

Assumptions provide a person with a sense of reality--which is only one of several possible realities--and values provide a basis for choice and evaluation. However, assumptions and values merge into one another. What is an assumption for one individual, or for one culture, may be a value for another individual or for another culture. Any one concept held by a person is likely to combine aspects of both assump-tions and values; hence it is difficult, and often unimportant, to de-termine whether it is one or the other.

In some cases the cognitive processes underlying cultural thinking are so abstract and lacking in substantive reference that they are probably best distinguished from assumptions and called "cultural forms." Examples include assumptions about time, space, essence, ener-gy, and logical process. Cultural forms tend to overlap with assump-tions and, to a lesser degree, values. For training purposes it is probably not critical to be able to make firm distinctions; consequent-ly, after the nature of forms, assumptions, and values is illustrated, these concepts will generally be treated under the label "value and assumption" or, where it seems more appropriate, "predisposition." Occasionally, "perspective" or "frame of reference" will be used with more or less the same meaning.

A frequent objection made to efforts to analyze any culture, and any attempt to describe a people according to broad generalizations, such as cultural characteristics, results in stereotypes. It is clear that people differ widely with respect to any particular behavior or value. Nevertheless, certain values and assumptions are dominant in, for example, American culture and are shared to one degree or another by most members. Thus when we speak of an American value (or assump-tion), we refer to a peak or modal tendency for a range (distribution) of that value in the culture. All points on the distribution can be found in any society; thus when two cultures are compared on a given dimension, there is overlap (i.e., some members of Culture A will be more typical of Culture B than many members of Culture B who may be far from the modal point of their culture).

In addition, an individual's reactions will vary from situation to situation, and from time to time in the same situation. However, there is a _relative_ internal integration and stability in behavior over time and situation. Variations, thus, should not obscure syste-matic differences which do exist or the validity of stereotypes (modal tendencies) in understanding intercultural phenomena.

Derivation of Contrast Cultures

The simulation model calls for American values, assumptions, and cultural forms to be represented in the _spontaneous_ role-playing of the American trainee. The behavior of the person playing the advisor's

47

counterpart, on the other hand, is only semi-spontaneous, since he is
to be trained to respond in a way that will reflect contrasting values,
assumptions, and cultural forms. The strategy required that a conceptual profile which would provide a plausible contrast to the American
profile be developed as a guide for the auxiliary. These profiles are
summarized in Table 1.

Table 1

Summary of Cultural Assumptions and Values

American	Contrast-American

1. Definition of Activity

    a. How do people approach activity?
       (1) concern with "doing," progress,
          change-------------------------- "being"
       (2) external achievement------------- spontaneous expression
       (3) optimistic, striving------------- fatalistic
    b. What is the desirable pace of life?
       (1) fast, busy----------------------- steady, rhythmic
       (2) driving-------------------------- noncompulsive
    c. How important are goals in planning?
       (1) stress means, procedures,
          techniques---------------------- stress final goals
    d. What are important goals in life?
       (1) material goals------------------- spiritual goals
       (2) comfort and absence of pain------ fullness of pleasure and
                                 pain
       (3) activity------------------------- experience
    e. Where does responsibility for de-
       cisions lie?
       (1) responsibility lies with each
          individual---------------------- function of a group or re-
                                 sides in a role (dual
                                 contrast)
    f. At what level do people live?
       (1) operational, goals evaluated in
          terms of consequence------------- experiential truth
    g. On what basis do people evaluate:
       (1) utility (does it work?)---------- essence (ideal)
    h. Who should make decisions?
       (1) the people affected-------------- those with proper authority
    i. What is the nature of problem-
       solving?
       (1) planning behavior---------------- coping behavior
       (2) anticipates consequences--------- classifies the situation
    j. What is the nature of learning?
       (1) learner is active (student-
          centered learning)-------------- learner is passive (serial
                                 rote learning)

2. Definition of Social Relations

———————————————————(Continued)———————————————————

48

Table 1 (Continued)

Summary of Cultural Assumptions and Values

American	Contrast-American
a. How are roles defined?	
attained------------------------------	ascribed
loosely-------------------------------	tightly
generally-----------------------------	specifically
b. How do people relate to others whose status is different?	
(1) stress equality------------------	stress hierarchical ranks
minimize differences-------------	stress differences, especially to superiors
(2) stress informality and spontaneity--------------------------	stress formality, behavior more easily anticipated
c. How are sex roles defined?	
similar, overlapping------------------	distinct
sex equality--------------------------	male superiority
friends of both sexes----------------	friends of same sex only
less legitimized----------------------	legitimized
d. What are members' rights and duties in a group?	
(1) assumes limited liability--------	assumes unlimited liability
(2) joins group to seek own goals----	accepts constraint by group
(3) active members can influence group---------------------------	leader runs group, members do not
e. How do people judge others?	
(1) specific abilities or interests--	overall individuality of person and his status
(2) task-centered---------------------	person-centered
(3) fragmentary involvement----------	total involvement
f. What is the meaning of friendship?	
(1) social friendship---------------- (short commitment, friends shared)	intense friendship (long commitment, friends are exclusive)
g. What is the nature of social reciprocity?	
(1) real only-------------------------	ideal and real
(2) nonbinding (Dutch treat)---------	binding
(3) equal (Dutch treat)--------------	unequal
h. How do people regard friendly aggression in social interaction?	
(1) acceptable, interesting, fun-----	not acceptable, embarrassing

3. Motivation

American	Contrast-American
a. What is motivating force?	
(1) achievement----------------------	ascription
b. How is person-person competition evaluated?	

Table 1 (Continued)

Summary of Cultural Assumptions and Values

American	Contrast-American
(1) as constructive, healthy----------	as destructive, antisocial

4. Perception of the World (World View)

   a. What is the (natural) world like?
      (1) physical---------------------------- spiritual
      (2) mechanical------------------------- organic
      (3) use of machines-------------------- disuse of machines
   b. How does the world operate?
      (1) in a rational, learnable, con-
          trollable manner------------------ in a mystically ordered, spiritually conceivable manner (fate, divination)
      (2) chance and probability------------ no chance or probability
   c. What is the nature of man?
      (1) apart from nature or from any
          hierarchy------------------------- part of nature or of some hierarchy (<u>dual</u> contrast)
      (2) impermanent, not fixed, changeable   permanent, fixed, not changeable

   d. What are the relationships between man and nature?
      (1) good is unlimited----------------- good is limited
      (2) man should modify nature for his
          ends----------------------------- man should accept the natural order
      (3) good health and material comforts expected and desired-------------- some disease and material misery are natural, expectable
   e. What is the nature of truth? goodness?
      (1) tentative (working-type)---------- definite
      (2) relative to circumstances--------- absolute
      (3) experience analyzed in separate components dichotomies------------ experience apprehended as a whole
   f. How is time defined? Valued?
      (1) future (anticipation)------------- past (remembrance) or present experience (dual contrast)
      (2) precise units--------------------- undifferentiated
      (3) limited resource------------------ not limited (not resource)
      (4) lineal--------------------------- circular, undifferentiated
   g. What is the nature of property?
      (1) private ownership important as extension of self---------------- use for "natural" purpose regardless of ownership

5. Perception of the Self and the Individual

--(Continued)--

Table 1 (Continued)

Summary of Cultural Assumptions and Values

American	Contrast-American
a. In what sort of terms is self defined?	
(1) diffuse, changing terms-----------	fixed, clearly defined terms
(2) flexible behavior-----------------	person is located in a social system
b. Where does a person's identity seem to be?	
(1) within the self (achievement)-----	outside the self in roles, groups, family, clan, caste, society
c. Nature of the individual	
(1) separate aspects (intent, thought, act, biographical background)------	totality of person
d. On whom should a person place reliance?	
(1) self-----------------------------	status superiors, patron, others
(2) impersonal organizations----------	persons
e. What kind of person is valued and respected? What qualities?	
(1) youthful (vigorous)---------------	aged (wise, experienced)
f. What is the basis of social control?	
(1) persuasion, appeal to the individual---------------------------	formal, authoritative
(2) guilt-----------------------------	shame

Generalized Forms

American	Contrast-American
a) lineal--------------------------(time)	nonlineal
b) efficient and material cause-and-effect thinking----------------(space)	formal causes, correlative thinking
c) material, substantive------------------ --------------------essence and energy)	spirit, energy
d) operationalism (implied observer)-----	direct apprehension or formalism (dual contrast)
e) induction---------------------------	deduction or transduction (dual contrast)
f) judgment by comparison----------------	judgment against an absolute standard
g) world stuff expansive (unlimited good)	world stuff restricted (limited good)

Contrast-American culture, it should be remembered, represents divergent positions on the cognitive dimensions on which the American cultural profile has been plotted. In most instances, American culture profile has been plotted. In most instances, American culture may be described as lying at one extreme of the dimensions used, and the derivation of the contrast is relatively straightforward. On a few impor-

tant dimensions, American culture appears to have more than one contrasting position. In these cases it was not always clear whether the
three cultural positions in question could be plotted at points along a
single dimension. A number of such "dual contrasts" appear in Table 1.

To accommodate derivations of this sort, two similar but partially
distinct cultures were delineated. These are referred to as Contrast-
American I and Contrast-American II. The nonshared contrasts making up
these roles are described in Table 2. They can be seen to represent
either variations on a dimension in which the American position is in
the middle, or more complex contrasts (e.g., deduction vs. concrete,
Chinese-style transduction vs. American induction; theoretical compre-
hension vs. direct apprehension vs. American operationalism) which do
not easily fit on a single continuum.

Table 2

Differences Between Contrast-American Cultures I and II
Relative to American Culture

Measure	Contrast-American Culture I	Contrast-American Culture II	American Culture
Values and Assumptions	Delocalized group decision-making; integration (harmony) with natural world; euphoric attitude toward existence and reverence for life; past and future seen as expansions of present; commitment to concrete and phenomenal objects, syncretism of beliefs, a more complete unity always sought; existence is indeterminate.	Decision-making is a function of roles; self hierarchically differentiated from others by means of role; self linked to past via traditions; predatory, aggressively hedonistic approach to present existence; world is an abstraction known only through rules and tradition (formalism); people and things perceived as an explicit hierarchy; existence is an epiphenomenon.	Decision-making and responsibility localized in self; self separate from others and from natural world; group is not a unity but an aggregate of individuals; optimistically change-minded; commitment to operationalism, action, and mastery over environment; lineal inductive thinking, geared to anticipation of consequences; world perceived mechanistically as series of problems in search of solutions; nonesthetic, comparative, and relativistic judgment of events; totality of world stuff apprehended as unlimited; existence is action (doing)
Behavioral Characteristics	Ego-constriction (self-control, little eye and no body contact, physical aloofness, subdued tone).	Ego-expansiveness (intense eye and body contact, physical intimacy, hyperbole, exaggerated tone).	Moderate ego-expressiveness (moderate eye contact, minimal body contact, moderate distance, moderate tone).

52

Because there seem to be inherent natural forms of cultures, certain cultural concepts have a better fit with some concepts than with others. Contrast-American Cultures I and II, as depicted in Table 2 (only nonshared contrasts are shown), represent partially arbitrary choices, since alternative positions could have been assembled according to several permutations. Nevertheless, they were put together in the described pattern because they seemed to form a plausible configuration of values and assumptions. This consideration is important in our role-playing innovation because credibility is necessary for full trainee involvement.

To further assure the plausibility of the two Contrast-American roles, certain appropriate behavioral characteristics were designated as part of the auxiliaries' roles. These also are outlined in Table 2. It should be noted that such behavioral characteristics, although easily observable, are often difficult to analyze in terms of underlying assumptions and values. Perhaps this is because their very specificity links them to events and situations in a way that makes generalization hazardous. In any case, such stereotyped and easily observable behaviors are judged to be not so adversely intrusive in intercultural functioning as the more subtle, pervasive, and often unrecognized assumptions and values; the latter have accordingly received more attention in this work.

Development of Role-Playing Scenes

Descriptive background material was developed to provide the role-player with a temporal and situational context. This included a briefing with general information about the country and the work situation and experience of his predecessor. The briefing was purposely kept sketchy to allow the trainee to project himself into the situation and thereby provide maximum freedom in defining his own role.

The trainee takes the role of an American advisor who has been assigned to assist a non-Western auxiliary on development projects in the counterpart's country. He believes that the auxiliary is also a role-player who has received instructions similar to his own. The trainee is provided, within a role-playing context, with some comments from a predecessor who conveys a picture of delayed progress in the development projects without portraying etiological factors or localizing blame. The trainee is left to interpret the predecessor's comments any way he wishes. While the predecessor's comments reflect a frequent American stereotype of non-Western counterpart, the trainee may minimize or reject the stereotype by attributing it to the misperceptions of the frustrated predecessor.

In addition, brief background information was written for six scenes which were selected for their likelihood of eliciting typical American behavior. The information in each scene was recast and rewritten until it reliably evoked the culturally derived behavior necessary to bring about the desired cultural contrasts in values and assumptions. Each scene was designed to highlight select predispositions judged critical for overseas performance. The scenes were intended to be given in a sequence, with each scene built upon the overall background material and occurrence of the preceding scene. Some success, however, has been achieved in using the scenes individually.

An Example of Contrast-American Dialogue

[The American, Captain Smith, is trying to convince his host counterpart, Major Khan (the contrast-American role-player), to introduce
leadership-training into Khan's army. After some jousting they get on
to the theory of leadership.]

KHAN: But leaders ... you talk about the principles of leadership ...
        these are alright on the paper. A person who is a leader, he has
        the principles, leadership is a part of his nature, of his being.
        He doesn't have to rely on a piece of paper or a movie to know
        what a good quality is, or what a principle of leadership is.
        He is born with it. It is a part of his integrity. That is on
        what he works. He knows it, he just knows it.

SMITH: I think almost all men have the qualities of leadership within
        them. I think it's a matter of developing them. Some people re-
        quire no development, and you, I'm sure, have required no devel-
        opment, because if you did, if you lacked leadership or some of
        these traits, you would not have been appointed to the rank of
        Major. And I feel this is probably true of the officers through-
        out armies around the world in the rank of Captain.

KHAN: No, development is of course important, but it comes through life,
        through age, by being a leader. Fighting in the battle, out in
        front, your leadership emerges.

SMITH: Well, we have a little different theory of leadership. We feel
        that leaders are not born completely, and we feel that almost
        any man can become a leader....

KHAN: Oh---

SMITH: .... He must study, he must work at it.

KHAN: You mean to say, if you have ten principles of leadership, you can
        pick up a man from the streets, you could make a leader out of
        him, if he learns this?

SMITH: You may.

KHAN: Ah. You must be remarkable people if everybody can become leaders,
        Captain Smith.

SMITH: Oh, not everyone does become leader.

KHAN: That's what makes the American so great....

SMITH: No, I think what has made America great is, we were blessed in
        our early years by freedom from foreign countries, our oceans
        gave us time to grow, to try new ideas, formulate new concepts,
        not only of industry, of trade perhaps, but also in smaller areas
        such as the leadership area.

54

KHAN: I know a little bit of your history, and your country is great
        because it had great leaders like Lincoln and Washington and
        Jefferson, yes, men born leaders, great men.

SMITH: Yes I think that certainly these are all great men, but I think,
        having read their biographies, that they did work very hard to
        develop their leadership traits.

KHAN: Oh yes, a man has to work hard.

SMITH: We, I don't think we quite hold that theory. Our theory that
        has developed over a long period of time, is that older people,
        the parents, have the responsibility for developing the child-
        ren. The captains have responsibility for the development of
        leadership traits within the junior officers.

KHAN: Our traditions are also ... in fact, they're much more older
        than yours, thousands of years, our leaders are leaders, that's
        how they do things.

SMITH: Well surely just because ... I don't mean to infer that the
        American way is the only way, or that it is the best way, I
        was merely proposing it to you because I have noticed what I
        would call a definite lack of leadership in some of your se-
        cond lieutenants.

KHAN: You are aware of this lack of leadership in my lieutenants? You
        find fault with them Captain Smith?

SMITH: I do not find fault with all of them, but I do find fault with
        some of the techniques which some of them have utilized.

KHAN: Ah.

SMITH: And I know that, if they are allowed to continue, that the effi-
        ciency in the duties they're performing or that their soldiers
        will be performing, will be reduced.

KHAN: What kind of techniques are they using which are not good?

SMITH: They have an inability, I think, to communicate with the non-
        commissioned officer and properly supervise the accomplishment
        of the task. They almost have the attitude that this work is
        the type of work in which I should not take part, I should
        merely stand by and watch....I know you have a great respect
        for General George Washington, and I should give this example:
        One time during the War of Independence, there was a sergeant
        with some military pieces that were stuck, he was standing by
        very neat and clean in his uniform, and cajoling his enlisted
        men, shouting at them to push harder to get this cannon out of
        the mud. General Washington rode by on his horse and noticed
        this situation and stopped. He did not have his rank on for
        he had a large cape over his uniform, as it was very cold and

55

had been raining, and he asked the sergeant what the problem was.
The sergeant told him, "Sir, the soldiers cannot get this cannon from the mud." So, General Washington dismounted from his
horse and he walked over and assisted the soldiers in pushing
the cannon out of the mud. Then, he walked over to the sergeant afterward and he said, "Sergeant, tell your commander
that General Washington has assisted your men in pushing the
cannon from the mud." Now I think----

KHAN: Perhaps there was an extra help....help was needed to push the
         cannon. General Washington was a very strong man. Yes. So
         this help was very timely. It was a very good thing.

SMITH: The moral that I would like to point out in this story is that,
         I agree with you sir, that General Washington, like Lincoln and
         Jefferson, was a very fine leader....but he realized in this
         situation that the sergeant was not assisting his men at a time
         when they really needed assistance, and that each of us, re-
         gardless of our work, rank, if the time comes when we are re-
         quired to physically assist our men for short periods of time,
         then we must do so.

KHAN: Yes I agree. We should always assist whenever help is needed.
         We must also realize that there are certain status, certain
         positions in life that man has to live it. He will be a big
         failure if he doesn't live up as a general. What is the good
         of having a person who is born a leader, or born a general, do-
         ing the lesser type of work? He wouldn't be doing justice to
         his own being, to his own existence. Yes, a man must retain his
         own integrity, his own position.

SMITH: I think that if General Washington continually pushed cannons,
         he would have violated a different trait of a leader, his re-
         sponsibility is to look out for the welfare of his men, and to
         tactically employ them and to accomplish his mission. And if
         he is performing the job of a private soldier, he cannot do this.
         But that particular story pointed out one of the very essential
         traits of a leader; that he is willing to assist his men and do
         anything that they are doing if it is really necessary.

KHAN: Perhaps, if he was not in a disguise; he was wearing a cape---if
         he was in his uniform of a general, he would never have come
         down from, dismounted from the horse. He would have waited
         there as a general. People would have gotten extra energy
         while pulling the cannon. They would have looked at him, that
         big, tall, towering general, sitting on a horse, they would have
         looked at him and derived all inspiration and strength from
         him, and then pulled out the cannon without his assistance. His
         very presence would have been enough. Yes.

SMITH: Perhaps this may have taken place. However, the point he was
         trying to make is the same point that I'm trying to make sir;
         that many times the presence of an exalted ruler or an officer

is adequate, but at other times it is not, and that regardless, as you have pointed out on several occasions, I have assisted with my hands on these projects, because there was a situation there that I thought just required help. I don't think that it lowers the opinions of soldiers if the officer gives some assistance on occasion.

KHAN: Yes. But you see Captain, one thing leads to another. Always we start with something small. The moment we resign to it, we say, it doesn't matter, it's such a negligible thing, it won't make much damage to my integrity, to my virtuous life; the moment you give in one place you know, it grows. It grows, yes.

SMITH: Do you think helping soldiers on an occasion could perhaps damage your virtuous life?

KHAN: Maybe today you do that, tomorrow you make a larger concession to something else. You lose your integrity of the person, as an individual, as a leader. You're not doing justice to your rank, to your status.

SMITH: I think with proper training, and with the training that you have received, that you manifest, that you would never do this. That you would perhaps help one day but the next day you would see that there is not a need for your help. And it is through such means as the training films and conferences with subordinates, that you develop these qualities within the leaders; that he knows when to help and when not to.

KAHN: Yes. Perhaps you, you say your people are not born natural leaders, you train yourself, an individual who is walking on the street or who is in the army; but we value our positions very greatly, very deeply. It is the whole thing of our life and we value it, because we know it is divine by God. And we won't be living in the laws of God if we do things other than what he had divined for us. Yes.

Training Adaptation of Simulation Exercises

While some learning undoubtedly occurs during the simulation exercise itself, some form of "feedback," guidance, or explanation is necessary for maximum learning. Of course, the simulation could be presented in a variety of ways.

The approach used in the current application of the simulation involved live interaction, with the trainees participating as role-players (as previously described) and/or as observers of the role-playing. Attention was called to what had occurred in the role-playing encounter through a post-simulation interview with the trainee and, if viewed by an audience, an interview with the auxiliary. The intercultural phenomena of the interaction were then analyzed and implications drawn for overseas performance.

When the simulation was viewed by an audience, an introduction was usually provided. The introduction covered essential points on

the mechanics of role-playing and also attempted to sensitize trainees
to the basic phenomenon of cultural differences in values and assumptions.

The interviewing of participants in the role-playing exercise was
an especially important component of the format. The interviewer
probed for motives, intents, judgments, and affective responses--first
the American's and then separately the "foreigner's"--occurring in the
encounter. The auxiliary remained in role, answering questions as if
he were actually reflecting on his encounter with the American advisor.
Frequently, the interview interaction provided examples of cultural
assumptions and values as fruitful as the simulation dialogue itself.

The example dealing with George Washington on a horse will serve
to illustrate the nature of the interviewing. The first objective of
the interviewer was to elicit from the American participant his perception of his counterpart: how he perceived the rationale and motives of
Major Khan when the latter commented on George Washington's behavior.
The next phase of the interviewing was to elicit an evaluation by the
American of his own accomplishments. In the specific episode, for example, the American was asked to evaluate the effect of the story of
George Washington on Major Khan. Did it make its point? Was it con-
vincing? At a more general level, the participant was also asked to
evaluate Major Khan and to predict how he would be able to work with
him in the future. Finally, the American would be asked to place himself in Major Khan's shoes, and describe the situation, the events that
transpired, and himself as he believed Major Khan perceived him. A
similar interview was then held with Major Khan, who maintained his
assigned Contrast-American role.

The last stage of each simulation involved an analysis and synthesis. The events occurring in the simulation and elaborated in the
interview were analyzed in terms of the concepts on which the Contrast-
American culture had been built. The episode of George Washington helping the sergeant, for example, was interpreted as reflecting the trainee's (and Washington's) commitment to get a job done. The trainee's
point in using the story was that a job had to be done and that George
Washington, being a good leader, was willing to assist in the operation.
Among other things, the story illustrates doing, the American belief in
the value of activity. The story, as told, also illustrates the American emphasis on equality, rather than status, and the depersonalized
characteristics of American culture; namely, leadership is part of getting a job done, not part of a person's essential nature.

In the perception of the Contrast-American the situation looked
quite different. The first response of Major Khan was acquiescence to
the American, but he quickly interjected a personalized frame of reference into the episode; namely, how strong George Washington was. This
focus on the "man" (as opposed to the "job") was rejected by the Amer-
can, who attempted to redirect the conversation to the need for assistance. As the American persisted in pursuing his point, Major Khan re-
vealed a position clearly different from that of the American, a position which, in fact, agreed with the conduct of the sergeant. At this
point, then, a contrast between the two views on leadership became more
overt.

For the American, a leader is a person who does certain things;
he participates, demonstrates, and instructs. For the Contrast-American, leadership is a state of being; the effect of the leader on his

men coming from inspiration of his status rather than from participation--he orders, he does not necessarily do. Implicit in this view of leadership is the idea that a man is born a leader and not made so by virtue of training or acquired skill.

The nature of the analysis and synthesis is best guided by what emerges in the scene itself. The elaboration and incisiveness of the analysis attempted depends largely on the judged level of sophistication of the class of trainees and the skill of the interpreter in perceiving the values and assumptions underlying the interaction.

Possible Negative Trainee Reaction

The requirement that the trainee adjust, innovate, or simply cope with issues in the simulation exercises, without prior indoctrination or guidelines for behavior, has been observed to evoke defensivenss and rationalized denials of the relevance or validity of the exercises. This reaction is to be expected since the earlier stages of learning typically involve an unfreezing of habitual ways of perceiving that the trainee has depended upon throughout his lifetime. Since the training exercises question the absolutism of these perceptions, it is not surprising that he becomes somewhat emotional and anxious.

Among the comments and criticism that can be expected are "Language is really the important thing," "This guy can't be for real," "These exercises are artificial," "The room is not conducive to the necessary atmosphere," and "He speaks English too well." Although all of these arguments contain a partial truth, the fact that they are marshalled at all may be interpreted to mean that a confrontation has taken place. Given the difficult and challenging nature of the experience and the high involvement of participants making these kinds of comments, the comments seem to represent a form of insurance against failure.

In another form of defensiveness, the auxiliary may be perceived by the trainee as harboring personal antagonism toward him. While the manifest behavior may "legitimately" be perceived this way by the culturally insensitive observer, any competition or hostility in the exercise actually stems from cultural underpinnings, not from individual efforts to create difficulty or gain advantage over the trainee.

In one intensive training effort with a small number of military volunteers, all of whom were participating role-players, the trainees were allowed during an early stage of the exercises to ventilate defensive reactions such as those described. The trainer avoided challenging the statements but acknowledged the stressful nature of the encounter. Gradually the tenor of the comments and the overall attitude toward the exercise changed markedly. Some rather sheepishly admitted that it was "tough going," others said that it would certainly be too much for "naive second lieutenants" (the trainees were all the rank of captain or above), and still others acknowledged that they were taking the problems home with them. One trainee admitted that he had had an argument with his wife because she had questioned the credibility of a "non-Western" who spoke such fluent English. Also, at least one trainee held informal discussions with friends and associates (including his superior officer) on how to approach his counterpart in the simulations.

When the simulation is presented before a group of trainees with only one or two members of the class actually playing a role, additional issues of group response must be considered. The audience may identify solely with the "disadvantaged" American role-player and perceive no integrity in the Contrast-American role, or the audience may identify with the "unsophisticated" foreigner at the mercy of the "advanced" American. Either identification, if exclusive, tends to destroy a major training purpose of the simulation: to examine the cultural predispositions of an American while simultaneously drawing attention to the potential hazards underlying intercultural communication.

Variations in Conduct of Training

The intercultural simulation exercises offer considerable flexibility and versatility as a training technique. For example, they may be used as a dramatic beginning designed to "unfreeze" the trainee and set the stage for future learning. The primary intent of such an approach would be to increase his awareness of the possible limitations of his own cultural frame of reference and of the possibility of alternative ways of perceiving a situation.

At a much later stage of training, the simulation can serve as a behavioral "testing ground" and as an opportunity to achieve greater integration of knowledge ("refreezing"). This stage involves two types of inputs. One consists of the opportunity to experiment behaviorally and the other a greater understanding of the conceptual framework and ramifications of the cognitive variables being simulated. Exposure to alternative values and assumptions, together with dimensions that can be used to understand them, yields more transculturally valid perceptual sets (assumptions). This is especially true if the trainee has the opportunity to experience the "alternative" culture behaviorally, as in a role-playing exercise, as well as intellectually.

The level of interpretation of the simulation may also vary. For some role-players and observers, for example, the simulation is best considered as a practice or familiarization exercise, since the ambiguities and cognitive abstractions involved may make intellectual or emotional demands beyond their capability. For optimal training benefits, however, the trainee experiences a series of cognitive confrontations which, through a gradual loosening of cultural and personal moorings, lead to a more genuine acceptance of the relativism of American cultural values and assumptions. This process can be a taxing emotional experience. Uncertainty, doubt, and anxiety are familiar accompaniments, as are heightened vigilance and awareness.

Under these conditions, the postsimulation analysis takes on added importance. It appears imperative that a receptive individual ("interpreter") be available to assist the trainee to cope with his emotional reactions to his experience. In a sense, the interpreter must serve also as a cultural link between the trainee and the counterpart, providing the trainee with a sounding-board for his interpretations and reactions. This does not mean that the interpreter should pass direct judgment on such comments; usually a deeper involvement in the simulation is generated when prescriptions are avoided.

How, then, can the interpreter function to allow the trainee to get maximum benefit from the simulation experience? The answer lies

in the analyzer's ability to induce the trainee to examine crucial bits
of intercultural behavior and in encouraging cultural reality-testing
during subsequent exercises. In this way, the trainee is led through
cultural material at the depth and pace of which he is capable. In-
ferences drawn from the interaction are offered to the trainee according to his willingness to accept the integrity of the simulated behavior and his demonstrated need for codification. It should be clear
from these comments that the interpreter must give careful attention to
the trainee's emotional state, particularly his morale and resistance
to change.

With sustained exposure to the simulation exercises, a balanced
cognitive-affective approach must be assumed--that is, cultural attitudes or opinions must be seen in the context of a dynamic functioning
personality. This notion of the motivational context of attitudes is
not novel, having been emphasized by several writers in the last decade (e.g., Sarnoff and Katz, 31; Smith, Bruner, and White, 32).

Yet a third variation in the use of simulation devolves around
the engagement of single or multiple Contrast-American roles. Re-
peated meetings with a single-Contrast-American role-player establishes
a continuity of events and experiences. An increased interpersonal
involvement is generated, with an attending sense of obligation and
responsibility to an individual. However, instead of playing out the
scenes with a single counterpart, a trainee can be exposed to two (or
perhaps more) contrast roles for a particular scene before moving on
to the next scene. This procedure tends to throw the cultural dimensions into relief. By establishing a second point of reference in
one's "conceptual space," the technique facilitates the relativistic
interpretation of American predispositions. It would appear that
sacrifice of the advantages of the single-role approach would be jus-
tified when the simulation exercises are to be done before an audience.
It may also be preferred in other situations, but such judgments must
await actual experience with the roles used in this way.

Finally, variations in sequence and timing of scenes are possible.
For example, a single scene can be played several times, the number and
frequency of meetings being at the discretion of the trainee. This
technique should give the trainee more of an opportunity to show concrete signs of bridging the gap between himself and his counterpart,
that is, to act on his emerging understanding of the "foreign" culture.
The particular "solutions" developed by the trainee might be of interest in themselves as examples of superior adaptations.

Another alternate is to give all six scenes to the trainee at the
beginning and permit him to determine his own overall strategy. This
variation would significantly increase the burden on the auxiliary, who
would have to be prepared to offer contrast to a wide assortment of
assumptions derived from any of the six scenes or combinations of them.
However, the role-playing would probably seem more realistic, and effective integrative approaches to the problem may be developed by some
trainees.

ACTING THE CONTRAST-AMERICAN[1]

Cajetan DeMello

This actor was approached by a HumRRO research scientist to create a
role in a role-playing situation for a research project in cross-cultural
communication. The role to be created was that of a "foreign" national,
a counterpart of the United States Military Advisor stationed abroad. There
was to be no written script. The role-playing itself was to be spontaneous
and unrehearsed; and the character, consistent and realistic enough to be
believable. I accepted both. Any actor ought to be willing to explore
new vistas of artistic endeavors.

In order to understand and embody the character of the foreign
counterpart and subsequently to role-play in culturally-based simulated
encounters, I employed Constantin Stanislavski's system of acting of "psycho-
technique" to assimilate and role-play that character. What follows is the
study of an application of the Stanislavski system.

The research in the general area of intercultural, interpersonal
communication involving role-playing was undertaken by the Human Resources
Research Organization (HumRRO), Alexandria, Virginia. It was done under
contracts with the Department of Army.

My participation as an actor involved working principally with Dr.
Edward C. Stewart, Research Scientist. As the Leader of Work Sub-Unit AREA
III, he created the concept of the Contrast-American (a foreign counterpart
of the U. S. national abroad) character with its abstract culture. The role-
playing technique consists of simulating an encounter between an American
and his counterpart, the Contrast-American. The simulation[2] was used for
instruction and training which was conceived to enhance cross-cultural communication.

---

[1]Excerpts from an M.A. dissertation entitled, A Cultural Experience:
And the Art of Acting as a Technique for Simulating Cross-Cultural Interac-
tion through Role-Playing in Communication, Catholic University of America,
Washington, D.C., 1975.

[2]Simulation, in this study, refers to a socio-psychological representation of a natural phenomenon in which time is condensed and in which
cultural parameters (such as motivation, individualism, competition, etc.)
may be simplified or abstracted but their relationship remains unmodified.

Dr. Stewart was responsible for planning and developing the research program; Dr. Alfred J. Kraemer, Staff Scientist, served as the Work Unit Leader. Dr. Jack Danielian, Research Associate, developed role-playing situations (scenes) and testing instruments to assess the training implications of the simulation.

When Stewart left HumRRO in 1967, Kraemer took over the research and brought it to a conclusion. Under Work Unit COPE, he developed a programmed audio-visual instruction based on simulation exercises designed to improve intercultural communication skills.[3] The phase of the research discussed here is only the part under Stewart's direction.

For an actor to role-play, the Contrast-American was a real challenge since there was no dramatic character to recreate. The Contrast-American is an abstract character. He is a creature of the research scientist and is primarily created as a theoretical abstraction to provide a cultural contrast, serving as a mirror image if you will, to reflect American values in a cross-cultural encounter. The Contrast-American is derived from various cultures outside of the United States. He does not exist as a total being anywhere as such; but here and there, only in parts.

For an actor to role-play a Contrast-American effectively, he needs a concrete definition of the character. Being merely speculative is not at all helpful. It is valuable to have a theoretically descriptive concept of Contrast-American, but unless an actor has specific ideas and images of the state of being and the nature of a character, he is lost. He will have particular difficulty if he is instructed to engage in a controlled dialogue which will elicit from the American responses pregnant with American assumptions and values and American behavioral attitudes. He can and does make up things as the conversation progresses, yet he must in the first place have some kind of a framework in which to function.

If any culture comes close to that of Contrast-American, it is the culture of the people of India. The Contrast-American shares many of the cultural traits associated with tradition-oriented societies. He also has in common a pattern of behavior depicting characteristics which can be easily identified as belonging to Latin-American cultures. In other situations, cognitions[4] of Contrast-American behavior could be totally different, perhaps depicting traits that rightly belong to the cultures of the

---

[3]It is a program of videotaped segments (showing at least one cultural influence) of conversations occurring overseas between an American and host national. In all work situations, the part of the host national is played by me.

[4]"The term cognition is used here very broadly to refer to the processes of perceiving, recognizing, conceiving, judging, and reasoning." and to a person's values, assumptions, ideas, beliefs, and modes of thought. See footnote of Alfred J. Kraemer, "A Cultural Self-Awareness Approach to Improving Intercultural Communication Skills," (a paper presented at the Annual Meeting of International Studies Association, New York, March 1973), Professional Paper 5-73 (Alexandria, Virginia: HumRRO Division 7, April, 1973), p. 1.

Arab world. Nonetheless, in every situation, Contrast-American would exemplify social and cultural mannerisms quite different, and in many cases, opposite to those of the American. Hence, one can say that Contrast-American is an evolving character. He becomes as he role-plays. Given a few fundamental truths of life of family, social position, profession, etc. the actual reality of his existence takes on form and shape in each and every role-playing situation.

Unlike a subject-role-player (usually a U.S. national) who relies on his own personal idiosyncracies and experience in his performance as Captain Smith, an actor-role-player portraying Major Khan, Contrast-American, does not. On the contrary, an actor-role-player is deliberately constrained and is required to perform in accordance with the nature of the research. He is directed and trained by the researcher to bring out culture-worthy materials which will be of maximum value for educational and training purposes. In fact, an actor has to refrain from his own attitudes and views except when they coincide with Contrast-American's way of life.

It is important to bear in mind that cultural norms and mores of Contrast-American are not arbitrarily contrived as part of a contrasting cultural environment. The style and the conditions of life of Contrast-American are valid. The politics, the economics, the religious beliefs, the value system and other traditions attributed to Contrast-American are based on numerous authoritative research studies and authenticated by field work. Not all of these activities, whether manifest or subtle, come into play each time in every role-playing situation, nor is every opportunity seized by an actor to present an opposite view. Much depends upon the talent of actor-role-player who is expected to engage in a realistic and spontaneous rapport with the subject-role-player. Nevertheless, the cultural contrasts are there and do manifest themselves whenever a conversation stimulates their preeminence.

Since we are dealing with role-playing in a simulation and not with a character in a play, all we can do is to predict a certain behavior on the part of the American-role-player and formulate creative objectives of desired expectation. The scenes are written with the objectives for training purposes inherent in them. For example, in scene 3, one of the training objectives written into the scene is on the notion of publicity along with a rationale for the same: " . . . You / Captain Smith/ have determined that publicity of the existing projects is indicated. Such publicity should do much to neutralize suspicions and swing public opinion behind the community development programs." A creative objective calls the actor-role-player to lead the American in a conversation to draw forth his idea of publicity and to have him explicate his desire and the need for it. Thus, one can say that creative objectives are the same as training objectives which evidently are based on research.

A description of the role-playing simulation in progress will reveal the various things that the actor has to concentrate on and the creative process at work--to the extent that it is explainable.

Very early during the period of preparation, it became clear to me that in order to be most effective as a role-player, I would have to experienc things in life consciously as a Contrast-American, to the extent possible. I should be so thoroughly steeped in the character that it should be possible for me to step in and out of the role at will. Therefore, for a substantial part of the day, I began to live so to speak as a Contrast-American character--mentally, psychologically and experientially, in order to become knowledgeable of the American way of life by contrast. From daily conversations with my American friends, colleagues and people, I consciously familiarized myself with the style of their language. A scene in a movie, a passage in a novel, television programs and commercials, newspaper advertisements and other items, articles in magazines, all would fire a spark of learning, great imaginings, and create a reservoir of knowledge for me, and prompt a behavior towards an American; all in the inner life of the character's being. And I would long to be engaged in a genuine conversation with my Captain friend feeling supremely confident to deal with him whenever an occasion demanded. In this manner the Contrast-American saw the world with my eyes, felt it with my senses, perceived and became aware of it the way I wished myself to be as a role-player for the role.

As I bequeathed all of my personal awarenesses and historical past to the Contrast-American, by the end of one year of preparation and numerous role-playing simulations, the Contrast-American and I had merged into one being--assimilated one into the other. The degree of assimilation was so intimate that my own person and my character could not be distinguished. Though distinct and separate personalities, we were comfortably and desirably entrapped within one human form.

> . . . Bring yourself to the point of taking hold of a new role concretely, as if it were your own life. When you sense that real kinship to your part, . . . your newly created being will become soul of your soul, flesh of your flesh.[6]

However, in ascribing to the Contrast-American, my own activities and observations, there was one fundamental reservation. While it was of utmost importance for me as an actor to have the knowledge of the American's predispositions, perceptions and sensitivities, it would have been futile for the character of the Contrast-American to have such a highly informed and enlightened awareness. I had to draw a line where the actor-person would cease to be and the actor-role-player would begin to exist. In the early stages of role-playing, the drawing of this thin line posed a dilemma. However, with much practice the dilemma was overcome. This was done mainly by listing related concepts which may appear in the conversation, and by predicting American behavior, to the extent possible, in the given situation. Yet, I must confess that whenever the dilemma persisted, it was to the detriment of effective role-playing performance.

Every role-playing exercise is a unique experience because of the newness of the subject-role-player. As he expresses himself, an actor-role-player, in keeping with the research perspective, strives to maneuver the subject-role-player to expose his social and cultural manifestation to enhance training in cross-cultural communication through self-realization. A similar kind of self-awareness takes place in the observer-participants because of empathy which leads them to a vicarious experience. The manipulation is not done at the sacrifice of the validity of the role or the role-playing simulation. Though the actor's performance is deliberately structured, it is incumbent upon him to be natural, his manner unforced and his deliberation very real.

---

[6]Stanislavski, An Actor's Handbook, p. 12.

DEVELOPMENT OF A CULTURAL SELF-AWARENESS APPROACH

TO INSTRUCTION IN INTERCULTURAL COMMUNICATION

Alfred J. Kraemer

Preliminary research

To explore various approaches to increasing cultural self-awareness, video recordings were made of simulated intercultural encounters. These were role-playing encounters in which an American and a foreign actor pretended to meet in the context of a work situation in an imaginary foreign country. The actor had been trained to play the role of a host national in such a way as to reflect cultural influences that were in plausible contrast to certain influences prevailing in American society.[1] (The design of the encounters was a new version of an earlier model described by Stewart, Danielian, and Foster, 8, which did not allow for universal values and, therefore, contained sharper but less plausible cultural contrasts.)

About 80 persons, including military officers, Foreign Service personnel, college students, and businessmen, participated inthis research. The work situations were such that the participants could readily imagine actually being in them.

During playbacks of the recordings most role-players could recognize only the very obvious manifestations of cultural influences in themselves, in spite of the clues provided by the behavior of the actor. When their attention was drawn to less obvious manifestations by asking them to explain a given thought pattern, or a particular way of expressing the thought, the reasons given were almost invariably in terms of what they perceived to be the constraints of the situation (the imaginary one, as well as the role-playing situation), or in terms of their individual uniqueness ("I guess that's just the way I am, that's me").

The recordings were also shown to persons who were interested in the research, including psychologists, and others concerned with improving training for overseas assignments. With rare exceptions, their ability to recognize cultural influences in the Americans' behavior did not seem much greater. Again the focus was mostly on the individual characteristics of

---

[1]Descriptions of these influences can be found in the writings of DuBois (4), Fuchs (5), and Williams (6), and in the collection of writings edited by McGiffert (7).

the role player and on assumed situational constraints. As French has noted, "in certain contexts, all behavioral scientists know that we too 'have a culture.' Far less frequently is this culture made part of explanations of our own behavior. It is a function of the culture bondage we all share that we 'forget' our own culture, even after having become intellectually convinced of its existence." (9, p. 420). The difficulty in recognizing the influences of one's own culture does not seem to be caused mainly by lack of knowledge that there are certain cultural influences in American society. (Reading a book on American culture would not help much.) Instead, the difficulty appears to result primarily from the fact that these influences manifest themselves only in combination with other influences, such as education, age, occupation, role, group membership, or situational constraints. In addition, most people rarely have any need or opportunity to learn to recognize the influences of their own culture, while learning to recognize the other influences is part of the socialization process.[2]

The observations made during the preliminary research led to certain conclusions concerning the design of a learning experience in which one is confronted by behavior that could easily be one's own.[3] Second, the experience should be structured in such a way that one would learn to perceive cultural influences in spite of the presence of other influences. Third, it should involve the learners actively in the learning process; they should actually be practicing the analytic behavior required for the recognition of cultural influences.

Small-group exercise

These considerations led to the design of a small-group exercise in which participants are shown video recordings of staged segments of conversations between an American and a host national in an imaginary "non-Western" country. The roles are played by actors, and the dialogue follows a script. The segments appear to be excerpts from recordings of spontaneous conversations, but only these excerpts were written and produced. Each shows at least one manifestation of a cultural influence in what the American is saying, or in the way it is said. The excerpts are grouped into sequences, with each sequence showing several different manifestations of a given cultural influence, while the other influences vary from excerpt to excerpt. Thus, in any one sequence, a particular cultural influence is a common element that is gradually brought into focus. Participants in the exercise view one excerpt at a time. After each one they try to form a tentative hypothesis--in writing--as to the cultural influence (or influences) reflected in what the American is saying. They then discuss their hypotheses. Their task is to learn how to discover the common cultural element in each sequence. The instructor's function is to facili-

---

[2]In behavioristic terms, learning to "recognize the influences of their own culture" refers to learning discriminative verbal responses to certain characteristics of Americans (including oneself). In the language of attribution theory, it refers to a change in one's perception of the causality attributed to these characteristics.

[3]Ideally, one should be confronted by one's own behavior. However, a technique that would accomplish this would be too expensive for most training programs.

tate the learning process.[4]

Selection of cultural influences

No research could be conducted to determine empirically what aspects of American culture should be included in the exercise--that would have required an additional major project--and no previous research suggested which aspects should be selected. For these reasons the selection was a matter of judgment, resulting in the following decisions:

(1) Well-known pervasive cultural values (e.g., individualism, egalitarianism, and universalism) were included.

(2) Certain cultural influences that seemed less likely to arise in the course of official duty overseas (e.g., those related to courtship, marriage, and sexual relations) were excluded.

(3) Certain elements that, although not generally recognized as cultural, are quite pervasive (e.g., aspects of decision-making processes) were included.

(4) Aspects usually referred to as "customs and habits" were omitted. (The fact that these are not universal is broadly recognized.)

It should be noted that it is not the purpose of the exercise to transmit knowledge of the existence of these aspects. In fact, it is assumed that participants who are not already aware of the existence of certain pervasive cultural elements in American society would benefit little from the exercise. It would be too difficult for them.[5] Nor is the purpose to transmit knowledge of the selected manifestations of these aspects. They are but a minute sample of the infinite possibilities. The purpose of the exercise is to develop the participant's ability to recognize a great variety of manifestations of these cultural influences, not just the few which appear in the excerpts.

The following aspects of American culture were selected:

Individualism--The belief that each person is a distinct entity and ought to assert and achieve independence from others.

Egalitarianism--The belief that all human things are equal in their intrinsic worth.

Action orientation.

Perception of interpersonal encounters primarily in terms of their immediate utility, and downgrading of the social significance of such encounters.

---

[4] A detailed description of the procedure to be followed during the exercise will be contained in an instructor's handbook which is in preparation.

[5] Unfortunately, they are unlikely to recognize this fact because the subject matter of the conversation in the excerpts is deceptively simple, and therefore readily understandable to them.

Universalism--The value attached to being guided in one's actions in a given situation primarily by an obligation to society (i.e., by general standards of conduct--laws, regulations, rules, established procedures, etc.).

Definition of persons (including oneself) in terms of their work and achievements.

The belief that the collective wisdom of the group is superior to that of any individual.

The idea that the process of decision-making requires evaluation of the consequences of alternative courses of action, and selection of the one that, on balance, seems most advantageous.

The belief that competition is a good way of motivating people.

The idea that there is usually a best way of doing something, which should be determined and then followed.

The belief that knowledge gained through observation is superior to knowledge gained in other ways.

Unnecessary quantification--The tendency to quantify aspects of experience that require no quantification.

Placing a higher value on utilitarian aspects of experience than on aesthetic ones.

Problem orientation--The tendency to perceive "problems" in the world, and in one's existence in it, and to look for "solutions."

The belief that thoughts cannot directly influence events.

Reasoning in terms of probability.

Impatience--The tendency to be annoyed by the pace of activities, if it is slow by one's own standards.

The tendency to make comparative judgments.

The willingness to offer one's services for the benefit of "the common good."

The belief in the existence of a behavior pattern called "self-help."

The use of absurd suppositions to communicate ideas or to elicit ideas from other persons.

Participants are not given the contents of the list.[6] For them the task is somewhat like learning how to solve crossword puzzles. Knowing the contents of the list, and their order in the exercise, would make the experience of viewing the recordings like that of looking at puzzles that have already been solved.

Of course participants need not use the same labeling or phrasing that appear in the list. Their own way of describing a cultural influence is sufficient--perhaps better. Some will have difficulty in expressing their discovery of a cultural influence in any kind of coherent statement.

No attempt was made to select mutually exclusive cultural aspects of American society. To do so would have resulted in a very short list of aspects at a very high level of abstraction, such as the five value orientations described by Kluckhohn and Strodbeck (10). An effort was made to select aspects across a wide range or level of abstraction. As a result, while the term "manifestation" has been used to refer to a particular way in which an aspect might manifest itself (as shown in an excerpt), some of the aspects may themselves be thought of as manifestations of a higher order aspect, that is, one that is conceptualized at a higher level of abstraction.

The selection of the listed aspects of American culture for the exercise does not, of course, imply that they are present only in American society, or that they influence all Americans to the same degree. It is assumed, however, that their variability within American society is smaller than their variability among the nations of the world.[7]

Empirical evidence for this assumption is not available for each aspect on the list. Research that would support or refute it has not been conducted in each case. However, the author takes the view that the burden of proof is on those who assert that a given aspect is universal. In the absence of empirical evidence, and when no logical argument can be made for universality, the assumption of cultural variation seems to be the better working hypothesis. For persons participating in the exercise the question of proof is not relevant. Much greater difficulties in communication can be expected to result from false assumptions of universality than from false assumptions of cultural variation. Since there is variation *within* American society, if some participants feel that a particular cultural aspect shown in the exercise is not reflected in their own cognitions, they can simply follow the dictum "If the shoe doesn't fit, don't wear it!"

---

[6]The order in which these aspects are listed is not the order in which they are shown in the exercise. The order was changed so that readers who might view the recordings could still have at least some of the experience they would have as participants in the exercise.

[7]The statistical definition of "cultural influence" implied by this statement was found to be more readily comprehensible to participants in the exercise than various anthropological definitions of culture.

Construction of Dialogue Excerpts

The following requirements were established as guidelines for the writing of the excerpts:

(1) The excerpts should give the impression of having been taken from ongoing conversations.

(2) These conversations should involve Americans of various occupations who are working overseas. (The military, the Foreign Service, the Peace Corps, and the oil business were selected. A description of the work situations is given in Appendix A.)

(3) The dialogue in each excerpt should make sense to the audience withtout connecting narrative.

(4) The dialogue should be plausible.

(5) The utterances of the host national should provide clues (i.e., indications of contrasting cultural influences) that help the participant discover cultural influences in the Americans' cognitions. (The requirement for plausibility prevented this from being done in all cases.)

(6) There should be a clue-providing utterance by the host national at or near the end of the excerpt. This would make it possible to vary the level of difficulty of exercise by either including or excluding these utterances. (Again, the requirement for plausibility prevented this from being done in all cases.)

(7) There should be a sufficient amount of noncultural content in each excerpt to serve as a distracting element, as would often be the case in real-life dialogue.

(8) In each sequence of excerpts, the behavior of the Americans should show a variety of manifestations of the same cultural influence.

It did not seem desirable, and it would in fact have been very difficult, to have each excerpt contain a manifestation of only one cultural influence. To attempt to do so would have caused each excerpt to be so brief that, in most cases, the dialogue would not have made sense without introductory narrative. The reason for this difficulty is that a single cognition often contains more than one cultural element.[8] Consequently, some excerpts could have been placed in a sequence other than the one in which they appear.

The following excerpt illustrates how the above requirements influence its construction. The context is a conversation between a Lieutenant Colonel Konda, the Deputy Director of Instruction at the host-country military academy, and a Major Smith who serves as an advisor at the academy.

Smith: No, no thank you, sir. I think I'd better be getting back to my office.

Konda: Yes, this has been a good meeting, Major Smith.

Smith: Yes, sir, it has. I think we've had a very good discussion. I understand your situation much better now. Your explanations were very helpful.

Konda: Yes, yes, a good meeting. We had a good talk, yes. We like your ideas, yes. You must visit again.

---

[8]A similar difficulty was experienced by Kluckhohn and Strodbeck in the construction of items for their value orientation schedule.

```
Smith:    Well, sir, I'm always glad to be os some help.  Per-
          haps we could get together when I receive the materials
          from West Point.  I could bring them over and show
          them to you.9
Konda:    Ah, Major Smith, why wait for the materials?
```

The first two "lines"[10] tell the audience that the excerpt is
taken from the final part of the conversation. The next two lines
contain distracting elements. Smith's last line reflects a cultural
influence that is common to all excerpts in the sequence, namely, the
downgrading of the social significance of interpersonal encounters. The
key sentence is "Perhaps we could get together when I receive the materials from West Point." It reflects Smith's idea of making his next encounter with Konda contingent upon the existence of a work-related reason for getting together, and implies that he sees little value in meeting without such a reason. Konda's last line provides a clue without
which the discovery of the cultural influence becomes much more difficult. If this excerpt is shown first in the sequence, viewers can, of
course, form only a tentative hypothesis as to the common cultural influence that they will be trying to discover in the sequence.

The following is another example from the same sequence. The context is a conversation between a Mr. Konda, who is in charge of the provincial office of the Ministry of Education, and a Mr. Smith, an American
oil company executive, who will be in charge of the training center at
a new refinery being constructed by the company near the provincial capital. Smith is concerned about getting applicants for the training program who have a minimum level of education. He meets with Konda to discuss this.

```
Konda:    Yes.  Next time you come, we can do that.
Smith:    Well, this has been a very useful meeting.
Konda:    Yes, yes, we are happy that you could be with us.  And
          now, before you go, Mr. Smith, you must meet the other
          men in my department.  They know about your oil company,
          building this new refinery, yes, yes.  I will go with
          you and you will meet them.
Smith:    Well, thank you.  That's very kind of you.  I hope it
          won't be too much trouble.
Konda:    Trouble?
Smith:    I mean, I don't want to take up too much of your time.
```

Some of the excerpts are considerably more difficult that the
above examples. A higher level of difficulty is illustrated in the following excerpt from another sequence. The sequence is relatively easy
since the cultural influence is well-know. The context is the same as
that of the last example.

```
Smith:    But we want to be sure that only the best qualified men
          get hired.
Konda:    Yes, you must have good men, of course.
```

---

[9]The dot indicates where the playing of the dialogue would be
stopped to increase the difficulty of the excerpt.

[10]"Line" refers to everything said by one actor without interruption.

```
Smith:    Yes, that's why we have to have the interviews and the tests.
Konda:    I see, and how will you know which are the good men?
Smith:    Well, we'll interview only those who do well on the tests, of
          course.
Konda:    I see.  But how can a man do well in the test when you have not
          yet hired him?
```

A final example will illustrate what is probably the highest level of difficulty. Not only is the excerpt difficult, but it is part of a sequence which deals with a cultural influence that is not well known. The context is the same as that of the first example.

```
Smith:    Yes, sir, very good.  Colonel Konda, has the general reached a
          decision as to which of the possible new courses he will add
          for next year?
Konda:    Yes, we will have that course you and I talked about last time.
Smith:    I see.  May I ask what determined the general's selection of
          that particular course?
Konda:    As you know, we have a new instructor--Major Bakka.  He is a
          good man, and he knows this subject.  So this will be the new
          course.
Smith:    But, sir, I believe you indicated that there were good instruc-
          tors for the other courses that were being considered.
Konda:    Oh, yes, yes, certainly.  But, as you know, we can have only
          one new course.
```

The video recordings contain 138 excerpts. Most of the 21 sequences contain seven excerpts each. The average length of the excerpts is less than a minute. The difficulty of the exercise may be increased not only by omitting clue lines, but also by omitting the easiest excerpts in each sequence.

Trial administrations of the exercise

At successive stages during the development of the exercise, portions of the recorded material were used in small-group settings with about 300 military officers, Foreign Service personnel, and businessmen. This was done to (a) determine the feasibility of the approach, (b) discover flaws in the excerpts that had to be corrected, (c) develop the instructional procedure, (d) determine the appropriate level of difficulty, and (e) experiment with various techniques of overcoming resistance to the learning experience. The following is a summary of what was learned during these trials.

Plausibility: In spite of the fact that the video recordings show staged performances, most viewers perceived the dialogue as natural and spontaneous rather than theatrical. Some of the groups were not told until after the exercise that the performances had been staged. Instead they were led to believe they would see excerpts from spontaneous conversations that had occurred during role-playing encounters. At the completion of the exercise, almost all the participants in these groups thought what they had seen was unrehearsed. Only a few were not sure. This is important because participants are more likely to accept the performances as plausible if they do not seem staged--even when they know that they are.

Group Homogeneity: An important requirement for the conduct of the exercise is that the participants' existing level of cultural self-awareness be similar. A great disparity makes it impossible to find an appropriate level of difficulty for the group. Participants for whom the level is too low have too little opportunity to learn; others for whom it is too high may get frustrated and aggressive. Unfortunately, cultural self-awareness does not seem to be related to the criteria according to which persons are grouped together in programs of instruction for Americans going overseas. It thus becomes necessary to make up new groups to conduct the exercise successfully. The cultural self-awareness test developed to evaluate the effectiveness of the exercise could be used for this purpose.

Prerequisites: The exercise is intended for use with persons who are emotionally suited for intercultural assignments, and who have certain minimum levels of intellectual ability and social science education. Just what these minimum levels are remains to be determined. Unlike students who have mistakenly entered a calculus class when they should be in a beginning algebra course, participants in the exercise may not realize for some time that they are out of place. This can happen because the dialogue in the excerpts is readily understandable to everyone who might be a participant.

Resistance to the learning experience: Negative reactions by at least one member of the group, usually in the form of irrelevant criticisms, are not uncommon. There may be participants who consider themselves quite sensitive to cultural differences but who, contrary to their expectation, find the exercise more difficult than most other persons in the group. This uncomfortable experience can result in disruptive behavior on their part. They may vehemently question the plausibility of the manifest content of some excerpts, or they may insist that the common cultural aspect of the Americans' behavior in a given sequence is universal. Some participants may react negatively because they cannot accept the fact that their own ideas and behavior are subject to influences over which they have no control. That reaction itself is undoubtedly determined, at least in part, by cultural influences.

Duration: The exercise, when properly conducted, lasts about two days. Usually only four or five excerpts per sequence should be used. The preparation of a group of instructors for conducting the exercise takes about three days, assuming they have a social science background and intercultural experience, and know how to conduct small-group instruction.

Does participation in the exercise actually increase one's cultural self-awareness? This question could not really be answered because no instrument for measuring cultural self-awareness was in existence. Consequently, a test was developed which could easily be administered to groups who had gone through the experience. Its development and the results of the evaluation of the exercise will be described in an instructor's handbook.

Excerpted from: Development of a Cultural Self-Awareness Approach to Instruction in Intercultural Communication. Human Relations Research Organization, Alexandria, Virginia, 1973. (with permission)

LITERATURE CITED

1. Brein, Michael, and David, Kenneth H. "Intercultural Communication and the Adjustment of the Sojourner," *Psychological Bulletin,* vol. 76, 1971, pp. 215.230.

2. Hartley, Eugene L. and Hartley, Ruth E. *Fundamentals of Social Psychology,* Knopf, New York, 1955.

3. Riesman, David. "Some Questions About the Study of American Character in the Twentieth Century," *The Annals,* vol. 370, 1967, pp. 36-47.

4. DuBois, Cora. "The Dominant Value Profile of American Culture," *American Anthropologist,* vol. 57, 1955, pp. 1232-1239.

5. Fuchs, Lawrence H. *Those Peculiar Americans,* Meredith Press, New York, 1967.

6. Williams, Robin M. *American Society* (2nd ed.), Knopf, New York, 1961.

7. McGiffert, Michael (ed.) *The Character of Americans* (rev. ed.), Dorsey, Homewood, Illinois, 1970.

8. Stewart, Edward C., Danielian, Jack, and Foster, Robert J. *Simulating Intercultural Communication Through Role-Playing,* HumRRO Technical Report 69-7, May 1969.

9. French, David. "The Relationship of Anthropology to Studies in Perception and Cognition," in *Psychology: A Study of a Science.* Vol. 6, *Investigations of Man as Socious: Their Place in Psychology and the Social Sciences,* Sigmund Koch (ed.), McGraw-Hill, New York, 1963, pp. 388-428.

10. Kluckhohn, Florence R. and Stodtbeck, Fred L. *Variations in Value Orientations,* Row, Peterson, Evanston, Illinois, 1961.

CHAPTER IV

THE CULTURE ASSIMILATOR

CULTURAL ASSIMILATORS

Henry Holmes and Stephen Guild

General Description. Cultural assimilators are, in essence, a programmed approach to learning about a culture. They have been developed by a group at the University of Illinois for training purposes. They can be obtained from this group or an experienced teacher could write his own.

This technique can be used individually by students without the direct help of the teacher. After completing several of the exercises, the class can discuss details of the cases and do further research if necessary.

Group Size. Can be used with any size group, but discussion afterwards should be in smaller groups.

Time Required. Varies. This depends on the individual student and on how much time is spent in discussion.

Materials Utilized. 1) Cultural Assimilators. 2) Paper and pencil.

Physical Setting. A normal classroom setting is adequate. Moveable furniture is desirable for discussion.

Process. 1) Hand out the cultural assimilator materials. Give students time to examine them and ask any questions they may have. 2) Students should go through the assimilator step by step according to the instructions. 3) When students are finished they may want to compare answers and discuss why they answered as they did.

Special Instructions. If one devises cultural assimilator type materials on his own, it is very important that their accuracy be checked thoroughly. Because of the type of materials, if there are inaccuracies, these can be misleading and can be more damaging than instructive. You should use the "Cultural Assimilators" already published before trying your own.

77

Resources. "Cultural Assimilators" for various countries can be obtained from the Group Effectiveness Research Laboratory, Department of Psychology, University of Illinois, Urbana, Illinois.

Examples. An Arab student asked his co-workers on his lab assistantship if they wanted to go to lunch with him at the Student Union. They agreed, adding that it was time to eat, and they all chatted as they went to the Union where they got in line at the cafeteria. When they reached the cashier's station, the Arab student, who was first in line, paid for all of them. When the group got to their table, his two co-workers insisted on giving the Arab student the money for their lunches. The Arab refused it, but the Americans insisted; and the one sitting beside him swept the money off the table and dumped it into the foreign student's jacket pocket. Later, the Americans commented that the Arab student had been unusually quiet and reserved while he ate his lunch.

If the Americans had analyzed this incident correctly they probably would settle on which one of the following explanations for the Arab's behavior during lunch?

1. The Arab student must have had an upset stomach. Go to page I. (see immediately below)

2. It is the Arab custom not to talk during meals. Go to page II. (see immediately below)

3. The Arab student had wanted to pay for their lunches and he was hurt that they wouldn't let him. Go to page III. (see immediately below)

4. The Arab student felt the Americans thought he was too poor to pay. Go to page IV. (see immediately below)

5. When he was away from the lab, the Arab had nothing to make conversation about. Go to page V. (see immediately below)

You chose 1: The Arab graduate student must had had an upset stomach.
    This is a bad choice. Apparently you missed a key point.
    A stomach upset can come on suddenly—but if it does, would one continue to eat and watch others do the same?

You chose 2: It is the Arab custom not to talk during meals.
    Somtimes people may want to eat in silence, but if such is their mood, why would they suggest that other people eat with them? While the members of some cultures do dine in silence, this is not the custom with members of the Arab culture.

You chose 3: The Arab student had wanted to pay for their lunches and he was hurt that they wouldn't let him. Right.

Most Americans would not, under the circumstances, interpret the Arab's invitation (an ambiguous word, isn't it?) as implying that he intended to pay for their lunches. However, in Arab culture, a suggestion that others join you in eating is an indication that you are inviting them to be your guests; it is a gesture of hospitality and generosity.

No wonder the Arab student was upset! As the situation evolved, it really was for the Arab basically a case of the guest's supplying their own food after they had accepted his invitation.

Aside from the confusion, the student must have felt over the apparent inconsistencies in the behavior of the Americans, he probably also felt that their behavior was deliberate rejection of his hospitality--and, therefore, of his friendship as well.

All over the world acceptance of generosity and hospitality involves a more or less rigid obligation to repay in an approximately similar form sometime.

A generous Arab, when thanked, may say, "Don't thank me; you will repay me someday."

An American refusing an invitation to be a guest is much more likely to say, "Let's go 'Dutch'."

You chose 4: The Arab student felt that the Americans thought he was too poor to pay for all the lunches.

Incorrect. You have overlooked significant information which should have indicated to you the correct information.

This thought may have passed through the Arab student's mind, but it would probably not be the first one, nor the one mainly dwelt upon. One of the other alternatives would provide a better explanation of the young man's behavior.

Re-read the passage, noting carefully what happens and how each of the people involved behaves toward the others at each point in the episode.

You chose 5: When he was away from the lab, the Arab had nothing to make conversation about.

Wrong. Your answer is inconsistent with the information given.

Since we've all met some people as narrow in their interests as this, is this choice culturally relevant?

Furthermore, this choice practically contradicts the situation as described in the passage.

Outside a classroom during a ten-minute break, several Americans and an Arab student were exchanging ideas about a project on which they were working. When they had first come out for the break, most of the Americans took out cigarettes and lit them. The Arab student watched them; then, hesitantly, he finally took out his pack of cigarettes and lit one. After the break had ended and they returned to their project work, the Arab student was very quiet, and he seemed slightly hostile when he did speak.

Which of the following do you think is the most likely reason for the apparent change in attitude on the part of the Arab student?

1. He had said all that he could. Go to page VI. (see below)

2. He didn't like the brand of cigarettes the Americans smoked and was contemptuous of their choice of cigarettes. Go to page VII. (see below)

3. He was reacting in a natural manner for an Arab student in an American university; i.e. his moods change quickly. Go to page VIII. (see below)

4. He was offended that the Americans had not offered him a cigarette. Go to page IX. (see below)

5. He thought the project work done after the break was silly. Go to page X. (see below)

Your answer was 1: He had said all that he could.
It is evident by your response that you have completely missed the point.
The incident indicates that the Arab student not only was quiet but he also showed signs of hostility. If he had just run out of ideas, would there be any reason to be hostile to the others?

Your answer was 2: He didn't like the brand of cigarettes the Americans smoked and was contemptuous of their choice of cigarettes.
No. Do not fall asleep on the job.
This is an incorrect choice. Would most people become hostile or withdrawn over other people's brands of cigarettes?

Your answer was 3: He was reacting in a natural manner for an Arab student in an American university; i.e., his moods change quickly.
A very poor answer. You are wrong.
It is not natural for an Arab first to be friendly with a group of people and immediately afterwards to be hostile and withdrawn. A change of this sort is caused. The question is: Who or what caused the change described in the paragraph?

Your answer was 4: He was offended that the American had not offered him a cigarette.
Good. This episode was fairly difficult. The selection of this alternative is indicative of good judgment.
This may seem like a trivial matter to an American, since Americans are used to buying and smoking their own cigarettes. But to an Arab, offering someone a cigarette or anything (e.g., food, drink, etc.) that you are about to enjoy yourself is only common courtesy, especially when you are in the role of host--no matter how broadly conceived the role may be. In this incident, for example,

in relation to foreigners, Americans are essentially seen as hosts
by the Arab student. An Arab would only neglect to offer a cigarette
to someone if he wished to show his dislike of the other person.

Your answer was 5: He thought that the project work done after
the break was silly.
What happened? That was not a difficult choice.
Perhaps he did, but is there a statement to this effect?

Excerpted from A Manual of Teaching Techniques for Intercultural
Education, University of Massachusetts, Amherst, Mass., 1971.

IRAN CULTURE ASSIMILATOR

Martin M. Chemers and Arlene G. Chemers with
Fred E. Fiedler, Lawrence M. Stolurow, and Harry C. Triandis

Instructions: The culture assimilator presents an incident or
a situation to you on one page and in paragraph form. Then you are
asked to select one alternative from the next page that is appropriate
to what is asked for as well as to the situation as presented. After
each alternative you will be directed to go to a particular page where
you will be given evaluative feedback on your response. If your
selection is not appropriate, you will be asked to make other selections.

You may sometimes feel that you do not have enough information to
make a sound selection. In such a case, consider carefully the information that is available, and then respond as best you can in the framework required by the question. After all, most tourists do not study
intensively the culture of every country they visit - yet they return
home with many definite reactions to the people and cultures that they
have been exposed to. The difference between the casual tourist and you
is that the culture assimilator presents you with the culture organized
in a pattern that is related to your goal; whereas, the tourist usually
meets culture randomly.

Although more than one alternative may seem appropriate to you
sometimes, you are to select only one at a time. From among the
alternatives listed, there is always one that is more appropriate than
the others.

Turn only to the page indicated. Read the passage attentively.
Analyze thoroughly. Build on past learnings. Work quickly but carefully. Whenever you make an incorrect response you will be directed to
return to the episode page. Re-read the episode carefully, looking for
information or clues you may have missed the first time, then select
another alternative.

(Editor's note: In order to save space, answers to the incidents
are printed immediately following. In the original assimilator they
were printed on separate pages for instructional purposes. Four examples of assimilator questions are included here.)

QUESTION ONE

    Ali and his young wife left his father's village home and headed
for a nearby small city where a new industry was being established.
Most of the people who were already living in the city were employed in
small businesses and the service trades, and thus were not available
for the new factory's labor force. So the new industry had sent repre-
sentatives out to many of the surrounding villages to recruit workers,
since most of the Iranian nation's population was rural.

    Ali, who had helped his father raise sheep, had no other specific
work skills, but he had attended the local school so he was the first
of his father's family who could read and write.

You should now proceed to the next page where a question and alternative answers are given.

A thumb-nail sketch of Ali would make it clear which of the following
probably is a statement of his main reason for leaving his father's
village home:

A. Ali and his father believed that going to the city to work in the
    factory offered a brighter future for the young man than tending
    sheep near the village did.
        Go to page _____

B. Ali and his father realized that the profit in sheep-raising was
    steadily declining, and it would soon not be sufficient to sup-
    port both families.
        Go to page _____

C. Ali and his wife both wanted to get away from the older folks,
    and going to work in the new city factory provided a good excuse
    for them to leave the village.
        Go to page _____

D. Ali has no proper sense of responsibility about helping his old
    father with his work, and so he considers only his own interests.
        Go to page _____

You chose A: Ali and his father believed that going to the city to work
in the factory offered a brighter future for the young man than tending
sheep near the village did.

    Very good. This choice is correct. There are several hints in
the passage that could be used to justify this choice.

    Since his father has sent Ali to school, he probably wanted Ali
to be better prepared for life than he had been. Further, Ali's liter-
acy wouldn't be fully utilized by tending and marketing the family's
relatively small block of sheep. Therefore, since both men are aware
of the nation's emphasis on the development of local industries, the
prospects for the future look brighter for the young in the area of in-
dustrial work than they do in the area of small-scale livestock raising.
        Go on to the next question ...

You chose B: Ali and his father realized that the profit in sheep-raising was steadily declining, and it soon would not be sufficient to support both families.

Incorrect. You have overlooked significant information which should have indicated to you the correct alternative.
Reread Question One and make another choice ...

You chose C: Ali and his wife both wanted to get away from the older folks, and going to work in the new city factory provided a good excuse for them to leave the village.

This is a bad choice. Apparently you missed the key point. This sort of situation may be the case when young couples live with their in-laws. However, in Moslem countries, the older people are shown great respect and deference by younger people. Therefore, the conditions in the household would have had to be quite unpleasant for the situation described in C to have occurred. Is this statement the main reason for the departure? Imagine how Ali and his family see the matter.
Reread Question One and make another choice ...

You chose D: Ali has no proper sense of responsibility about helping his old father with his work and so he considers only his own interest.

This choice is incorrect. Although many Iranian men may marry at relatively late ages, does the passage indicate that Ali's father is an old man, or that he is dependent on him? In addition, older people, especially parents, are traditionally treated with great respect. Reread Question One and make another choice ...

QUESTION TWO

Robert Allenby, an oil company technician, was being sent to Iran by his employers. In preparation for his trip he began to do some reading about the faraway land to which he was going. He had often heard about Persian arts, Persian rugs, and the Persian language. He also knew that at one time Iran had been known as Persia, but the name of the country had more recently been changed to Iran. This change in name caused Mr. Allenby some confusion.

Which of the following statements best explains the reason for the change in name from Persia to Iran?

A. The Allied Powers changed Persia to Iran at the time of their occupation of the country during World War II.
Go to page _____

B. "Iran" is a name which reflects the long history of Iranian civilation.
Go to page _____

84

C. "Iran" is a Persian word which means "source of power" and was
    adopted to lend importance to the country.
        Go to page ____

D. The importance of the change from Persia to Iran lies in its re-
    ligious significance.
        Go to page ____

You chose A: The Allied powers changed Persia to Iran at the time of
their occupation of the country during World War II.

    This answer is incorrect. The protective occupation of Iran by
the Allies took place during the period of 1941-1945. The national name,
Iran, was adopted in the 1930's. The influence of outside powers was
not a major factor in this decision.
        Reread Question Two and make another choice ...

You chose B: "Iran" is a name which reflects the long history of Iranian
civilization.

    Quite so! This is, indeed, the correct answer. The word Iran
means "the land of Aryans." The Aryans were an Indo-European people
who settled in this part of the world around 2,000 B.C. These Aryans
included several distinct peoples, among them the Persians, Medes, and
Parthians. The Persians settled in the area around the Persian Gulf
and there developed one of the greatest and most powerful civilizations
the world has ever known. Under several kings, including Cyrus, Darius,
and Xerxes, this empire spread over most of Asia carrying with it its
advanced civilization. This civilization was known as Persia, and the
name endured until modern times.
    Modern-day Iran includes many peoples who are not truly Persians,
such as Arabs, Medes, Baluchis, Kurds, Luis, Jews, and the descendants
of the Mongols. Thus, in the 1930's, the name of the country was changed
to Iran, to include all of the Iranian peoples, and to reflect the glory
of its ancient civilization.
        Go on to the next question ...

You chose C: "Iran" is a Persian word which means "source of power" and
was adopted to lend importance to the country.

    Incorrect. The word "Iran" does not mean "source of power." The
adoption of the name Iran has an important cultural significance of which
you are not aware.
        Reread Question Two and make another choice.

You chose D: The importance of the change from Persia to Iran lies in
its religious significance.

    This answer is incorrect. The word or name "Iran" has no reli-
gious significance, but it does have an important cultural one.
        Reread Question Two and make another choice.

QUESTION THREE

A team of five young <u>American</u> architects was working on the plans
for a shopping center. Each of them was supposed to design one part of
the shopping center as he wished, but in conformity with the already accepted master plan for the center as a whole.

At one of their staff meetings, Henry Andrews presented his drawings for comment and criticism. When he had finished, Marty Johnson,
who was also his close friend, talked for about 15 minutes about faults
in Henry Andrews' proposal and how they could and should be avoided.
Henry defended some of his points and conceded others. After the other
three had expressed their views briefly, the meeting was concluded.

As the group separated, Marty and Henry headed for the coffee
shop together, as they usually did after staff meetings.

If you were asked to explain the meaning of the behavior exhibited by
Henry Andrews and Marty Johnson, as it is presented in this passage,
which of the following would you select as the most probable explanation?

A. Both men are very ambitious to succeed and become famous, regardless of what it may cost them.
      Go to page ____

B. Both men see criticism of a man's work as different from criticism
   of the man.
      Go to page ____

C. Henry is a man of extraordinary self-control as shown by evenness
   of temper in the face of criticism.
      Go to page ____

D. Martin was of a considerably higher status than was Henry.
      Go to page ____

You chose A: Both men are very ambitious to succeed and become famous regardless of what it may cost them.

   <u>Incorrect</u>. This is not the best answer. There is no direct evidence in this passage to point out that either man was excessively ambitious. While ambition may have played a part in their behavior, there is
a more obvious and culturally relevant concept shown in the episode.
      Reread Question Three and make another choice.

You chose B: Both men see criticism of a man's work as different from
criticism of the man.

   <u>Correct</u>. Good thinking: One of the most important aspects of
American culture is brought out in this story. Every man performs in
many roles (for example as a worker, father, friend, member of a bowling
team, etc.). In American society these roles are kept very much apart.
For example, if a man has a good job and is rich (his work role), that
does not mean he will be elected captain of his bowling team (his
leisure role). Thus, a man sees his work as something separate from

86

his overall personal life. Therefore, it is possible to constructively criticize a man's work without criticizing him as a person. It is important to remember that not all societies treat their various roles in the same way as Americans do.

Go on to the next question ...

You chose C: Henry is a man of extraordinary self-control, as shown by his evenness of temper in the face of criticism.

Incorrect. Henry did not show any special self-control. In fact, it would be considered somewhat abnormal if Henry were to become angry at the constructive criticism offered by Martin. There is a better explanation for his behavior.

Reread Question Three and make another choice ...

You chose D: Martin was of a considerably higher status than was Henry.

Incorrect. The passage indirectly implies that all the architects were of equal status. Each one was designing an equal portion of the shopping center in accord with the master plan. Furthermore, in American culture, a man does not have to be of superior status to criticize a colleague's work. Status is not the important factor in this episode.

Reread Question Three and make another choice ...

QUESTION FOUR

Hassan, an Iranian foreign student, was working on a class project with several American students at a meeting of the project staff. The Iranian student was asked to give his suggestions concerning the way the project should be carried out. Immediately after he finished talking, Jim, one of the American associates, raised his hand and said in a clear voice that he disagreed with Hassan's proposals. Then he pointed out a number of specific difficulties that Hassan's approach would incur for the project as a whole and its staff.

After the meeting, Hassan told Jim and another student on the project that he would not be able to go to the movies with them as they had planned because he just remembered that he had to get a book out of the library to prepare for a class the next day. When the two boys expressed disappointment and suggested that they could go the next evening, Hassan politely told them that he already had another appointment for the next evening.

Assume that you were the other student who had planned to go to the movies with Jim and Hassan after the meeting. Which of the following thoughts would you regard as most likely to be a correct analysis of the situation as you went off to the movies with Jim?

A. Hassan was offended because Jim had disagreed with his ideas in front of others.

Go to page ____

87

B. Hassan did not like to mix work and pleasure and would rather not go out with his project co-workers.
   Go to page ____

C. Hassan had never liked Jim and wanted to have as little to do with him as possible.
   Go to page ____

D. Hassan did not think that it was polite to accept Jim's invitation at first, but would have gone if Jim had really urged him.
   Go to page ____

You chose A: Hassan was offended because Jim had disagreed with his ideas in front of others.

   Correct. This passage illustrates a cultural trait directly opposite to the one shown in the last passage. In Iranian culture, a man's various roles are not as clearly separated as they are in American culture. Thus, person and role are united. Hassan interpreted Jim's criticism of his proposal as a criticism of Hassan personally. Thus, he no longer wanted to be friendly with a man who had openly criticized him in front of others, lowering his status. Here you see one of the basic differences between the Iranian and American cultures: the separation or fusion of roles. Keep this in mind as you read on.
   Go on to the next question ...

You chose B: Hassan did not like to mix work and pleasure and would rather not go out with his project co-workers.

   Incorrect. You are using the concept which you learned in the last item, but you are applying it to a situation where it no longer applies. The Iranian concept of roles is quite different from our own. Keep this fact in mind while you look for the correct alternative.
   Reread Question Four and make another choice ...

You chose C: Hassan had never liked Jim and wanted to have as little to do with him as possible.

   Incorrect. If this were true, Hassan would not have previously accepted the invitation to go to the movies. The passage states that he has already accepted, but later changed his mind. The important question is "Why did he change his mind?"
   Reread Question Four and make another choice ...

You chose D: Hassan did not think that it was polite to accept Jim's invitation at first, but would have accepted if Jim had really urged him.

   Incorrect. You have shown some good thinking, but have gotten on the wrong track. This answer might be true, if this were the first time Hassan was being invited. However, it is stated in the passage that he had already accepted the invitation, but later had changed his mind.
   Reread Question Four and make another choice.

Excerpted from: Iran Culture Assimilator, Dept. of Psychology, University of Illinois, 1967 (with permission).

PROFILE OF CROSS-CULTURAL READINESS

U. S. Naval Amphibious School

Sure, you may be willing to try new things. Maybe you are the
type who is ready to try an exotic foreign dish.
But just how daring are you really? Are you courageous enough to
try new experiences in a whole new setting--such as Bangkok, Athens,
Tokyo? Fill out this profile and find out how ready you are to cope with
new experiences that are confusing, frustrating, and even maddening.
Read the following questions. Answer each one as you honestly believe you
would react. Choose only one answer for each question. (If you cheat,
you're only making it harder for yourself.) Then turn to the scoring section that follows to discover your "readiness" quotient. To draw in your
readiness profile, follow the directions at the end of the scoring section.

1. In a foreign port you are a passenger on a bus crowded with many people.
   You have to get off at the next stop. You signal the bus driver, and
   he slows the bus down, but doesn't stop. You jump off while the bus
   is still moving past your stop.

       a. You are puzzled and resolve to watch other people getting off
          buses to see how they signal the driver to stop.
       b. You shrug your shoulders and walk away.
       c. You become angry at the bus driver and yell a few foul words at
          the bus as it departs.

2. The oldest son of a local family invites you to his home to meet the
   rest of his family. Another guest, an elderly host national, arrives
   at the same time you do. You both enter the room where the family is
   waiting. The other guest greets the grandfather, then the father, and
   finally the son. It is now your turn to introduce yourself.

       a. You greet your host and hope he will introduce you to the rest of
          the family and the guest.
       b. You hesitate, then turn and greet the family in the same order as
          you saw the guest do.
       c. You notice that the other guest greeted the grandfather and father
          first, but you assume they have met before. You greet your host
          first.

3. You are in Athens and need to change some dollars to drachmae. You enter a store and show a twenty-dollar bill to the cashier and she jerks her head up and down as if (in your opinion) to say "OK." You hand her the twenty. She looks puzzled and hands the money back.

    a. You figure that she doesn't like Americans, give her a dirty look, and leave.
    b. You give her the twenty back again and add 50 cents for a tip.
    c. You find an English-speaking Greek to help you out of your dilemma.

4. You've invited an officer from the local navy with his family to your home for dinner. The food is prepared and ready by 7:30, but your guests don't arrive until 9:30. Your food is burned to a crisp.

    a. You don't say anything, but serve your guests their plate of burned food, thinking this will teach them not to be late.
    b. You are angry and tell your guests how rude they have been to you.
    c. You offer refreshments, suggesting that you all go out to your favorite restaurant. You tell them that you ruined the meal, and you're very sorry.

5. You want to take a picture of a child. You take out your camera, but just as you are about to shoot, an old man rushes over and starts shouting at you.

    a. You hesitate and decide not to photograph that child, but you look around for another subject.
    b. You are aware that the old man does not want you to take the photo. You can't understand why, but you apologize and put your camera away.
    c. You wait until you think the man can't see you, then snap the picture anyway.

6. You are an enlisted man visiting a holy temple and notice shoes lined up outside the door.

    a. You walk into the temple with your shoes on because it seems silly to you to take them off.
    b. You take off your shoes as you've seen others do and walk into the temple.
    c. You hesitate as you are about to enter, then decide not to go in because you don't want to take your shoes off.

7. You ask directions haltingly in a foreign language; the person you ask directs you to the wrong place.

    a. You decide that from now on it would be wise to ask two or three people for directions.
    b. You get very angry and assume that the man gave you the wrong directions on purpose. You resolve to avoid nationals for future advice.

c. When you end up at the wrong place, you assume that you asked the question incorrectly or you misunderstood when the man answered you. You decide to ask directions from someone who can speak English from now on.

8. You are out on a date with a girl from the village near your ship. It has been an enjoyable evening, and you think that she likes you. However, when you try to kiss her good night, she shoves you away and rushes into her house, slamming the door behind her.

   a. You assume that she is cold and anti-American.
   b. You realize that it must not be the custom in this culture to kiss on the first date. You plan to phone her tomorrow, apologize, and ask for another date.
   c. You assume that you have done something wrong during the evening, and she didn't enjoy the date as much as you did.

9. You tell a host national friend that you were promoted in rank, and he congratulates you by giving you a warm hug.

   a. You accept the hug and hug him back, thanking him for his congratulations. You offer to buy him a cup of coffee.
   b. You're startled, but you let him hug you. However, you are a bit embarrassed about it and your actions show it.
   c. Embarrassed, you push him away and assume that he is a homosexual.

10. You have been stationed at Greenoch, Scotland, for over a year when you receive PCS orders to New London. Some people from Glasgow (a few friends and some friends of friends) invite you to a restaurant there. You arrive and find a farewell party in your honor. There are flowers, music, and wine. One of the guests whom you have never met hands you a gift.

    a. You thank him profusely and feel pretty good about yourself and what you did while you were stationed in Scotland.
    b. You thank him but tell him that you can't accept it because we have prohibitions against that sort of thing.
    c. You thank him but later you make a point of asking one of your Scottish friends if this stranger is some kind of kook.

11. At a party at the home of a host national you are watching people do some local dances. Suddenly your host takes you by the hand and asks you to join the dancing.

    a. You get up reluctantly, stiffly try a few steps to please him, but quickly sit down again.
    b. You shake your head "no" because you don't want to make a fool of yourself.
    c. You get up, glad you've been asked to join the festivities. Even though you're not very good, you try all the steps and stay up for the next dance.

12. In a foreign port you board a bus, take your seat, and the person next to you smiles a greeting.

   a. You smile, nod, and say hello. You try to begin a conversation in the language of the country, even though you realize that your vocabulary is limited to only a few words.
   b. You smile back and nod hello, hoping the passenger won't want to talk to you.
   c. You look away, pretending you didn't see him because you don't want to try to talk to him.

13. You are about to enter a restaurant in a foreign city. Near the door is an old woman who looks as if she hasn't eaten for days. She rushes up to you with hand extended, begging for money.

   a. You press a coin into her hand, look at her, and wish her a good day.
   b. You push her aside and tell her to leave you alone.
   c. You toss a coin at her and go quickly into the restaurant, not looking back.

14. You are a white ET. You go on liberty with your friend, a black ET, to a Spanish town. In the local bar that caters to Americans you notice that there are only two kinds of music: Spanish and country-western. Your friend mentions to you that he wished the bar had soul music.

   a. You insist that the bar owner produce some soul music for your friend.
   b. You tell your friend he can either forget about the slight and groove on Spanish music or go back to the ship.
   c. You engage the bar owner in a discussion about music. In the course of the talk you point out to him that he might get more business if he included some soul records. You say you'd like to stay longer, but your friend is getting bored, and you leave together.

15. You are at a bar when you find you need to use the head. You ask a bartender to tell you where it is. He points to the exit. You walk outside and find no head, only the wall of the building. A number of men and some women are using the wall as a toilet.

   a. You are disgusted and decide to go back to your hotel.
   b. You decide to wait because you would be embarrassed to expose yourself. You go back to the bar.
   c. You decide that this is the custom, and you join the others at the wall.

16. You are walking to a near-by village when you come upon a couple going your way. The peasant woman is loaded down with baskets tied to her back, but the man walking with her is carrying nothing.

a. You walk up to the couple and offer to carry some of the load. The man vigorously shakes his head and motions for you to leave, which you do.
b. You go up to the man and yell at him, bawling him out for treating his woman like a packhorse.
c. Although you feel sorry for the woman, you assume this is the custom. You greet the couple and walk on, figuring it's not your place to interfere.

SCORING SECTION

Let's face it, this is not an actual psychological test. It is a training tool, intended to foster understanding of ourselves overseas. Relax and score yourself.

Certainty Level

Questions 1 and 2 indicate your ability to deal with situations which demand that you act in one way, while your feelings tell you something else. The greater your capacity to accept contradictory situations, the more you will be able to deal with the kinds of situations you will encounter during your travels. How much uncertainty can you take?

Question 1: Stopping the Bus

a. You're on.the right track if you start to put the blame on yourself. Observation will soon tell you that the bus driver never stops for only one passenger. Stay cool. Score yourself 3.
b. You're doing OK, but still not facing up to reality. We can't crawl back into our shells and expect problems to go away. They won't. Score yourself 2.
c. It might be a good idea for you to stay on the ship rather than going on liberty because this is only a mild frustration compared to others you may have to deal with. Score yourself 1.

1. a: 3
    b: 2
    c: 1

Question 2: Greeting the Elders

a. Although you noticed the guest's actions, you ignored the message telegraphed to you. You should have seen that elders here are greatly respected and receive the first greeting. Score yourself 2.
b. You were not only smart enough to follow the guest's lead; you realized that it is the custom to honor elders by greeting them first when entering a room. Score yourself 3.
c. Perhaps you don't know that the custom is to greet elders first. However, you shouldn't ignore the fact that the guest who preceded you did

greet the grandfather first. Your score is low: recognizing unfamiliar customs is crucial. Score yourself 1.

2. a: 2
    b: 3
    c: 1

Adaptability

Questions 3 and 4 test how fast you adapt to unfamiliar environments. How quickly can you readjust to new problems?

Question 3: Changing Drachmae

a. You sure jump to the wrong conclusions! An up and down nod that means "yes" to us means "no" to the Greeks. She was telling you politely that she couldn't change money. Score yourself 0.
b. Again, think before you move ahead. Her polite refusal to change the American money doesn't mean she wants a tip. She probably would be insulted if you gave her one. Score yourself 1 for not losing your temper.
c. Right on. Her nonverbal nod meant the opposite of what it means to us. Finding an English-speaking Greek to translate will clear up the confusion. Score yourself 3.

3. a: 0
    b: 1
    c: 3

Question 4: Late Dinner Guests

a. Well, at least you kept your mouth shut. Burned food, however, is not an award for a misunderstanding. Are you sure you made it clear what time you expected them to arrive? Score yourself 2.
b. Just because you think the dinner hour should be the same as it is back home doesn't mean it is. You are applying your American perceptions to unfamiliar situations. This attitude will probably make relations with host nationals more difficult. Score yourself 1.
c. Good coping strategy--it won't take you long to learn that misunderstandings are often caused by your ignorance of local customs. Dinner hours just aren't the same the world over. Score yourself 3.

4. a: 2
    b: 1
    c: 3

Self-Awareness

How aware are you of yourself? Do you know how others see you? Can you use that information to cope with difficult situations? That's what questions 5 and 6 are testing--self awareness, the ability to use information about ourselves in puzzling situations.

94

Question 5: Using a Camera

a. Well, you made the right connection between the old man and the camera. But before you take any more pictures, try to find out whether your subject wants to be photographed. Score yourself 2.
b. Your awareness helped you choose the best reaction to this situation. You're really ahead of the game if you blame the misunderstanding on your own ignorance of local customs. Score yourself 3.
c. In some areas picture-taking is great. In some areas it is taboo. In some parts of the world taking someone's picture is like capturing his soul. The old man's actions should have tipped you off. Score yourself 1.

5. a: 2
    b: 3
    c: 1

Question 6: Shoes Off

a. Just because something doesn't make sense to you is no reason to refuse to do it. What doesn't make sense to you makes perfect sense to the host national. Score yourself 1.
b. You're not only observant, but you are willing to accept strange customs. Maybe you didn't know that you are to take off your shoes before entering many holy temples, but you figured it out. Score yourself 3.
c. You shut yourself out from a lot of new experiences if you are afraid to go ahead and get involved. You were correct to hesitate, and you were aware enough to see the relationship between the shoes lined up outside the door and entering the temple, but your next step should be to use that information in coping with an unknown situation. This way you didn't get to see the inside of the temple. Score yourself 2.

6. a: 1
    b: 3
    c: 2

Interaction

Do you communicate effectively with people? That's what questions 7 and 8 are trying to find out. How did you score?

Question 7: Asking Directions

a. Now you've got the idea--devise coping strategies for yourself and you'll survive. By the way, you're sensitive, too. Wouldn't you have been embarrassed to admit your ignorance if you had been in the same situation? Score yourself 3.
b. Your assumption is wrong. You sure must be uptight about how people feel toward you. Turn the situation around. Have you ever been asked directions and not been quite sure how to answer? How many times did you go ahead and try to give directions anyway, even if you were wrong?

You don't want people to think you are a fool--at least, not until they try to use your directions! Score yourself 1.

c. In reality, this could be the case. You may have made a mistake in trans-lation. After all, trying to converse in another language is not easy, and you're bound to make mistakes. Don't give up trying to use the language. Score yourself 2.

7. a: 3
    b: 1
    c: 2

Question 8: Dating

a. Perhaps a brothel is the only place you'll find any female with that attitude. Did it occur to you that in her culture a good night kiss might mean much more than "I like you?" In some countries holding hands in public can mark a girl as a prostitute. Score yourself 1.

b. You won't lack company in foreign ports; you have the courage to try. You'll call her and maybe you'll get turned down and maybe you won't. You can be sure that your apology will count heavily in your favor. Score yourself 3.

c. Blaming yourself is one way to explain difficult situations, but they aren't always your fault. You will really lose if you don't try again. Chances are she enjoyed the evening as much as you did. Score yourself 2.

8. a: 1
    b: 3
    c: 2

Self-Respect

What is your opinion of yourself? Sometimes people are so hung up on what others think of them that they forget to see themselves. Is that your problem? All you need is a little self-confidence. Questions 9 and 10 measure your self-confidence quotient.

Question 9: Hugged by a Man

a. Your self-respect not only allowed you to accept the hug as it was given, but also return the affection in kind. You are now better off than you were before. Score yourself 3.

b. This is really a natural reaction to something as foreign to your culture as being hugged by a man. Unfortunately, your embarrassment was probably felt by your friend and that reaction hurt his feelings. Score yourself 2

c. You have very little respect for your ability to judge people if sudden-ly you suspect a friend of making a pass at you. Are you really that good-looking? Score yourself 1.

9. a: 3
    b: 2
    c: 1

a. You have every right to feel good. Parts of your tour were tough, but
   now you are going home and that's great. You obviously were well-loved
   by many people and that's great, too. Score yourself 3 points. You're
   living proof that not all Americans are ugly Americans.
b. Come on, now. This man is paying you a big compliment. Dont' insult
   him by refusing his gift. Take another look at yourself. This group
   thinks you are great. Score yourself 0 for self-respect.
c. You did well to accept the gift, but you created bad feelings when you
   asked a Scottish friend if the stranger was a kook. Whether or not your
   question gets back to the stranger, you were overly suspicious. This
   Scot would call you "dour." Score yourself 1 point for accepting the
   gift.

10. a: 3
     b: 0
     c: 1

Initiative

If you are open to new experiences, willing to risk on a few adventures of
your own, you are loaded with initiative. How did you score on the initiative questions, 11 and 12?

Question 11: An Invitation to Dance

a. You get some brownie points for at least trying. Wouldn't it have been
   more fun to stay on your feet and try a few more steps? Score yourself
   2.
b. Well, you won't make a fool of yourself, but you won't win many friends
   either. However, this is a fairly normal reaction, although it does
   demonstrate a lack of initiative. Score yourself 1.
c. You not only have initiative, but you have self-confidence too. You
   realize that the host nationals expect you to try, and you carry it off
   as best you can. To show you have the right spirit, you even take on
   the next dance. Score yourself 3.

11. a: 2
     b: 1
     c: 3

Question 12: Talking to a Stranger

a. In this case you score extremely high on initiative. Not only do you
   acknowledge a stranger's greeting, but you also begin a conversation in
   the language of the country. A gold star for you. Score yourself 3.
b. This is the normal reaction, although your initiative quotient is definitely too low. If you're this afraid to use the language, you'd better
   do some boning up now while you have the time. Once in foreign ports, you
   will have to use the language or you will be less able to function. Score
   yourself 1.

c. Your reaction is really very insulting to your seatmate. The least you can do is nod a greeting or smile back at him. If you're going to "make it" in a foreign port, you'll have to be more courageous. Score yourself 0.

12. a: 3
     b: 1
     c: 0

Empathy

How aware are you of other people's feelings? How good are you at viewing things through another person's eyes? Empathy is the name of this quality. How did you score on questions 13 and 14?

Question 13: Dealing with Beggars

a. Good for you. Responding to beggars is not easy. There is always the temptation to pretend that they aren't there or to toss them a coin over your shoulder. But by looking at the woman and saying something to her, you can make her feel like a human being who deserves your respect. Score yourself 3.
b. Certainly an old woman can't be that big a threat to you! If you don't want to give her any money, OK, but try to find a less unfeeling way of refusing her. She's only the first of many that you'll meet on your travels. Score yourself 0.
c. Actually this reaction scores extremely low on empathy. By not even looking at the woman, you are telling her that she is somewhat less than a person. Better work on your style for saying no. Score yourself 2.

13. a: 3
     b: 0
     c: 1

Question 14: Music at the Bar

a. It's to your credit that you think of your friend's feelings. While the Spanish-speaking bar owner owes nothing to White or Black Americans, he does need their business. It is not in our best interests if he serves only one group. But maybe you can do more than just make a scene. Score yourself 2.
b. Make a little more effort to understand your friend's position. Put yourself in his shoes and think how you would feel going on liberty to places where Whites get consistently better service than Blacks, even before the money is on the bar. Score 0 and find time to do some reading and some thinking too.
c. You've come up with a cool solution to the problem. You thought of both your American friend and the host bar owner. Sounds like you'd be a great person to go with on liberty. Score yourself 3.

14. a: 2
     b: 0
     c: 3

Acceptance Level

How willing are you to accept things that are different? Without a certain amount of tolerance, you may find it hard to adjust to life overseas. How did you score on questions 15 and 16?

Question 15: Head at the Wall

a. You can be sure many of the host nationals wish that they, too, could go to an expensive hotel where the bathroom facilities are clean and the water is hot. However, there may come a time when you can't wait--what happens then? Score yourself 1.
b. This is a very normal reaction for Americans who have been brought up with certain standards about privacy and cleanliness. You will probably come around to using the wall when you see that no one pays any attention to what you are doing. Why should they? Score yourself 2.
c. Your acceptance level is high. That's good because you will need it if you are planning to do much traveling in out-of-the-way places. Score yourself 3.

15. a: 1
     b: 2
     c: 3

Question 16: A Heavy Load

a. Yes, it was the gentlemanly thing to do, but totally ineffective. There are customs all over the world that just can't be changed by you, so don't hassle it. Score yourself 2.
b. Chances are she has never heard of women's lib. You feel you have to protect her, but what if she is happy with her lot in life and even considers it an honor to serve her husband? The couple appear happy; this should tell you something; it should tell you to leave well enough alone. Score yourself 1.
c. This is really the best attitude to adopt. Your greeting shows that your tolerance level is high. You'll be far less frustrated in overseas settings if you are able to tolerate different standards of behavior. Score yourself 3.

16. a: 2
     b: 1
     c: 3

YOUR TOTAL SCORE IS _____

==

Are you ready to serve overseas and to go ashore? What are your chances of having an enjoyable time in an overseas port without offending or misunderstanding host nationals? Add up your total score and rate yourself with this scale. If your total score was between:

<u>48 and 46</u>: Excellent! You will not have many problems adapting to the
culture and your experiences ashore should be exciting and re-
warding. When new situations arise, you should be able to handle them
and find them challenging. When you return to the United States you will
probably miss your host country and the many friends you made there.

<u>45 and 34</u>: Good, but there is room for improvement. You will have some
difficulty adapting to the new culture. You will experience
some stress and confusion and will want to avoid some situations. Although you might want to have friends from the host country, your friends
may end up being mostly Americans. However, you could make some effort to
become more aware of your actions and how they affect others. Then you
would be quite comfortable in port.

<u>33 and 22</u>: Not good. You may already have had trouble in new places.
You may long to return to the United States and may have a
very difficult time feeling at home in port. In fact, you may avoid new
situations altogether and prefer only American friends. Often you will
be by yourself. You have too little confidence in yourself. Try to learn
more about the customs of the culture you are entering, how the host nationals view you, and how you can communicate with them. To begin with, learn
a few phrases from the host language. Visit any Navy ICR specialists in
the area. You still have time to make this tour a winner!

<u>21 and 12</u>: Danger! Better not leave the ship without more training and
advice. The way things stand now, you're bound to get in
trouble ashore and be just miserable. If you want to change, read this
manual and try to improve your score on this test. Try to learn some
phrases in the host country language. You've heard the saying, "Don't
just stand there, do something." Well, in your case it might be better
to just stand there and do nothing when you come upon a confusing situation that you don't understand. With patience and some very hard work
on your part, you might begin feeling more comfortable in port. In fact,
if you are careful to think before you act and if you try to accept the
different ways of the host nationals, you may begin to enjoy going ashore.
The PAO, your chaplain, your division officer, and our Navy ICR teams are
ready to make this a more satisfying tour for you.

Where do you need improvement? If you're an average American going
abroad for the first time, you need to develop skills which will help you
adjust to the new environment. With the chart on the next page you can
find out what your weaknesses are. Each spoke on the wheel represents a
skill or quality that is required for a successful adjustment in an overseas port. Each pair of questions in the test you've just taken tells
you how to rate yourself in that skill. Add the two scores for each pair
and then indicate your score with a dot on the appropriate spoke. For example, if you scored 3 on question 6 and 2 points on question 5, your
score for self-awareness is 5. On the spoke marked "Self-Awareness" put
a dot where 5 appears. After you've recorded all your skills, connect
the dots. The shape you draw is your readiness profile. A perfect score

would form a perfect circle at the end of the spokes. Does your score form a perfect circle or is your wheel squashed on a few sides? If it is, it won't roll very far. Round it out by trying to improve your overseas skills. Then you're ready to roll!

What skills do you need to improve?

certainty level	adaptability	self-awareness	interaction
self-respect	initiative	empathy	acceptance level

CULTURAL READINESS PROFILE
HOW WELL-ROUNDED ARE YOU?

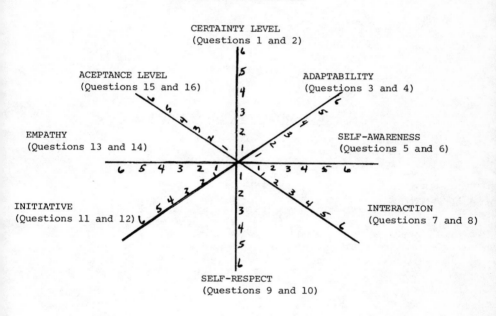

Excerpted from Overseas Diplomacy: Guidelines for United States Navy. (with permission)

CHAPTER V

<u>SELF-AWARENESS INVENTORIES</u>

SELF-ASSESSMENT INSTRUMENTS IN CROSS-CULTURAL LEARNING

Lowell A. Ingram

Self-Assessment of Leadership Skills

At the outset of a training program, trainees are asked to place
on a sheet adhesive tabs upon which are printed skills which have been
determined to be important for the trainee to possess when facilitating
a cross-cultural group. When given the tabs, the trainee is asked to place
on the continuum his/her responses as to his/her capability with the skills.
Words which the trainee does not recognize or understand should be placed
on the lines under "I have no knowledge or understanding of the following."

Trainees are encouraged to share their profiles with others in the
group for feedback purposes. This works best, of course, if the trainees
are known to one another before the training session. If they are not,
however, feedback may easily take place on their skills as trainees become
involved in using the skills mentioned on the tabs.

The skills identified on the tabs presumably are those which the
trainees must have a working knowledge of at the conclusion of the training session. Therefore, the trainer will carefully cover each skill and
trainees will have an opportunity to use them in practice exercises, etc.

At the conclusion, each trainee is asked to repeat the self-
assessment exercise, using a second profile sheet, thereby providing a
check on the degree to which the trainee has progressed during the training program. It also provides the trainer with a measure of his/her success
or failure with the training group in terms of training objectives, etc.

The words selected for use on the tabs may vary widely, determined,
of course, by the objectives of the training program.

The instrument could also be used in an Intercultural Communication
Workshop group to provide a profile and feedback exercise for the participants as they practice communication and perception skills in the group.

Example terms for tabs:

authoritative	listening	caring
honesty	teamwork	democratic
decision-making	creativity	paraphrasing
confidence	evaluating	use of exercises
self-knowledge	perception	nonberbal cues
self-motivation	sensitivity	gestures
assumption-checking	repeating	eye contact

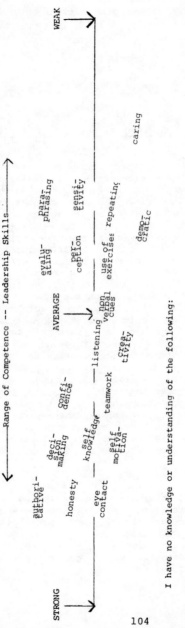

SAMPLE PROFILE

SELF-ASSESSMENT

of

LEADERSHIP SKILLS

<------ Range of Competence -- Leadership Skills ------>

STRONG   AVERAGE   WEAK

authori-
tative

honesty

eye
contact

deci-
sion
making

self
knowledge

confi-
dence

self
motiva-
tion

teamwork

crea-
tivity

listening

non
verbal
cues

evalu-
ating

per-
ception

use of
exercises

para-
phrasing

sensi-
tivity

repeating

demo-
cratic

caring

I have no knowledge or understanding of the following:

gestures

1. _____

2. assump-
tion
checking _____

3. _____

4. _____

5. _____

L. Ingram 3/75

104

Self-Assessment of Attitudes and Feelings

At the outset of a leadership training session (or Intercultural Communication Workshop), a profile sheet is given to each trainee. They are told that they will be given a series of words which have been printed on adhesive tabs. They are to take each tab and place it on the instrument in the place which best describes his/her initial emotional response at the time it is read; it should be placed according to free-association, first emotional response--as much as possible--without reflection on specific individuals or events.

The various areas on the instrument are then carefully described:

(a) AREA OF IGNORANCE (no contact)

Have had no contact with the term whatsoever and therefore are completely ignorant of it. Exposure through mass media, etc., would preclude placing a tab in this zone.

(b) MOST POSITIVE

The word on the tab evokes close, warm and the most positive of feelings.

(c) MOST NEGATIVE

The word evokes very negative feelings. If a tab is placed at the point of "most negative," it would indicate a total rejection of the word.

(d) LINE OF AMBIVALENCE

If a tab is placed on this point, it means a response of indifference-no opinion one way or the other, neither negative or positive.

Tabs may be placed at any point along the continuum from most positive to most negative. However, the inner circle or "Comfort Zone" represents feelings that indicate an acceptance into one's own "life space" and of course, if placed at the tip of the arrow at "most positive" represents total and unqualified acceptance.

The trainees are instructed that the exercise is completely private and they will not be asked at any time to share the completed profile with anyone. If an individual chooses to share the profile for feedback or other purposes, this is acceptable.

At the conclusion of a training program or ICW, participants are asked to again do the exercise with a second profile sheet, using the same tabs, thus providing a comparative study of one's possible change in attitude or feelings.

The hypothesis here, of course, is that there is a direct correlation between time and exposure and effective learning about a concept or culture and one's feelings and understanding about it.

105

The words used in the exercise may vary according to the type and purpose of training. The example given in this writing were those used with a group of Canadian trainees who were expected to have contact with at least 15 of the terms during their training. The variables for terms which may be used are many; cultures, values, etc., may be used in a wide variety of ways.

The pre-tests and initial uses of this instrument proved to be a valuable exercise for the trainees and, if nothing else, they stopped to think about how they view certain aspects of the world in which they live.

Example terms for tabs:

foreigners	Arabs	Eskimos
family	Americans	Afro-Americans
nationalism	Italians	Chinese
freedom	Jews	Native Canadians
honesty	Koreans	Latin Americans
God	Japanese	Africans
Canadians	French-Canadians	East Indians

and Feelings

Profile Sheet

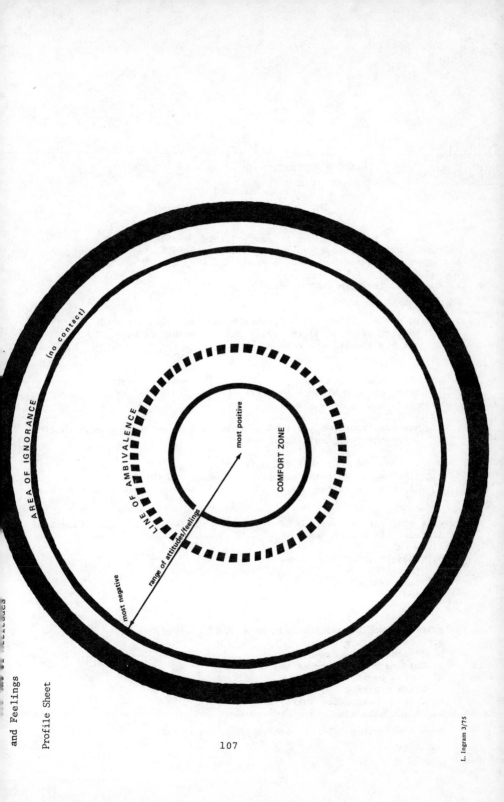

AREA OF IGNORANCE

(no contact)

LINE OF AMBIVALENCE

most negative

range of attitudes/feelings

most positive

COMFORT ZONE

107

L. Ingram 3/75

TOWARD A DEFINITION OF TERMS - AND MYSELF

Dianne P. Rood

Each of us is a unique product of this phenomenon we call
culture. Please jot down your thoughts on the following questions,
and we will discuss them when you have finished.

1. What does the term CULTURE mean to you?

2. a. Do you describe yourself, when asked, as belonging to a
      particular nationality, religious, or ethnic group? If so,
      can you isolate any reasons why?

   b. What experiences have you had that increased or deepened your
      sense of belonging to a certain group?

   c. How does your own particular background of cultural identification
      influence you, regarding:
      1) how you spend holidays?
      2) how you court(ed) and marr(ied)?
      3) how you express yourself - verbally and non-verbally?
      4) how you regard and behave toward other groups - preferences,
                                                          prejudices?

3. What experiences have you had with persons of cultural identification
   differing from your own?
   a. work?
   b. social?
   c. travel?
   d. friendships?
   e. media?

4. Briefly describe your concept of each of the following:
   a. Norwegian farmer
   b. Japanese businessman
   c. Chicano migrant worker
   d. Jewish banker
   e. Black preacher
   f. Irish construction worker
   g. Indian militant

   From what sources did you evolve these concepts?

5. Have you ever experienced any communication problems/breakdowns/
   barriers because of differences of yours and the other person's
   cultural background? Do you feel uneasy in such situations?

6. How do you measure the effectiveness of   communication? What
   can each person do to INCREASE the effectiveness of a communication
   situation?

CHAPTER VI

WORKBOOK APPROACHES

APPROACHING LIVING IN A NEW CULTURE

Jim McRae, Richard Vittitow, and Debra Mipos

WHERE ARE YOU?

      Learning to live and work in a new culture is a uniquely personal
experience. The way that the society is organized, what happens in a
group, the expectations and meanings people have for each other are all
probably different than in your own culture. And you will have to find
new ways to navigate through these unknown waters so that your needs will
be met. The rest of the workbook will help prepare you for that task.
Here, at the start, we need to look at the fears and hopes that we are
each taking into the new culture. Each person has his or her own set of
fears, hopes, and past experiences. It's amazing, sometimes, how similar
these are from person to person, but the important thing is to be aware
of your own unique set. The biggest step in becoming free of your fears
(and hopes) is to acknowledge and express them. Once they are acknowledged it becomes much easier to go beyond them--if they aren't expressed,
they have much more power to control us (and for much longer than we like
to admit).

      You've all heard stories about others' experiences about going to
another culture, and probably have your own opinions about why some people
succeeded well in a new culture and others didn't, and whether you will or
not. Reflect on all of this in answering the following:

A. What's the worst thing that can happen to you in adjusting to this new
    culture? (Also list your major fears and concerns.)

    _____

    _____

    _____

B. What's the best thing that can happen to you in adjusting to this new
    culture? (Also list the other things that you're excited about, or are
    looking forward to experiencing in this new culture.)

    _____

    _____

    _____

C. List the important experiences that you've had with other cultures or
    "people of difference."

    _____

    _____

    _____

Now and after completing each section or part, share as much as you wish with the rest of your group and discuss what you've learned by doing that section or part.

YOUR OWN CULTURE AND VALUES

Part A. Learning from Childhood

Our most intensive language and cultural learning takes place in childhood. At that time, we are taught among other things how to meet strangers and how to relate to them. Remember that you will be a stranger to people of the new culture. Reflect back on your own childhood and think about some of the things you were taught about strangers and people of difference-different ethnic groups, different religions, etc. When, where, and how did you learn these attitudes? Who taught them to you? To help you start on this, think of the first time you remember seeing someone different from yourself--what happened? What did you feel like?

Teachings about strangers and/or people of difference:

_____
_____
_____

Especially important is what you learned in childhood about people of the new culture. Think back and jot down all you can remember hearing about the other culture and its people--before you were twelve years old:

_____
_____
_____

Part B. How will Others see You?

(1) You'll be a stranger in the new culture. But not a neutral stranger--you'll be a specific foreigner--an "Indian," a "Japanese," or. . . . People of the new culture will react to you as such and expect   you to act like their image of an "Indian," a "Japanese," or . . . . This preconception may last a lot longer than you may expect-- parts may last until way after "they get to know you." It's important to be aware of this preconception and your image of it. Look through the following list of adjectives and mark through those that you think a member of the new culture would expect a member of your culture to be like, and pick out the five major ones:

Formal	Dependent	Trusting
Independent	Calculating	Competitive
Talkative	Warm	Masculine
Close	Tense	Spontaneous
Shallow	Reserved	Open
Serious	Frank	Impulsive

Cool	Distant	Cooperative
Relaxed	Deep	Feminine
Evasive	Suspicious	Responsive
Silent	Humorous	Dependent
Self-Assertive	Cautious	
Informal	Indifferent	

Summarize and add any aspects that you felt were left out of the list above so that the image that you think they have of people of your culture is expressed adequately:

_____
_____
_____

(2) How do you see your own cultures' values? Go through the same list of adjectives and mark those that you think fit members of your own culture in general, i.e., which adjectives express how members of your culture tend to be in comparison to people of the other cultures of the world. (Think of yourself in a foreign country hearing only that a member of your culture is coming to visit you--what would you expect that person to be like--as a best bet). Also pick the major five:

Formal	Trusting	Distant
Independent	Competitive	Deep
Talkative	Masculine	Suspicious
Close	Spontaneous	Humorous
Shallow	Open	Cautious
Serious	Impulsive	Indifferent
Dependent	Cool	Cooperative
Calculating	Relaxed	Feminine
Warm	Evasive	Responsive
Tense	Silent	Dependent
Reserved	Self-assertive	
Frank	Informal	

Summarize and add any aspects that you felt were left out of the list above, so that the image is complete:

_____
_____
_____

Part C. Your Own Values

In going to a new culture you take with yourself the history, values, and attitudes of your own culture. Individuals rarely get beyond or outside the range of their own cultural systems. It's important to have a clear understanding of your own culture, so as to know what others are reacting to and what you are acting from. However, you are not just a representative of your culture--you occupy a unique position within it. And

it will be you, with your own specific (and perhaps changing) set of
values, identity, needs and interests who will be interacting with the
people of the new culture. The better sense of your own values, identity,
and needs you have, the better you will be able to move freely and adopt
new behaviors and give up old ones,around your core identity. The following experience is designed to help you gain a sense of your own values.

Who Am I? Instructions to be given out one at a time.

First-- on each of ten small pieces of paper write a short (one word or
       phrase) answer to the question "Who am I?" (i.e., you'll have ten
       different statements that complete the phrase "I am . . .")

_____

_____

_____

Second--go through the ten pages and on each write a few sentences about
       what that answer means to you; what turns you on about that part
       of yourself.

_____

_____

_____

Third--arrange the ten sheets in order of priority--from the one that you
       feel is most important to you to the one which is 10th most im-
       portant.

_____

_____

_____

Fourth--read through all that you've written and see if there are any
       major themes, trends, or values which appear in several of your
       answers. Jot those down on the rest of this page.

_____

_____

_____

LOOKING AT NEXT YEAR

Part A. Prediction of the New Cultures Values

     Another of the important things that you are taking in to your new
situation is the set of expectations that you have. What do you expect--
or think--that you will do there? What will the people there be like?
How different will it be from your own culture? We often carry the pre-
conceptions we have of what the new culture will be like around with us
a lot longer than we realize. Because they affect how we feel and act,
it's important to start with an awareness of what we expect to find. To
help get a hold on this expectation set look through the following list
and mark all the items that you now think fit the new culture and its

114

people. Also decide which five are the most important ones:

Formal	Trusting	Distant
Independent	Competitive	Deep
Talkative	Masculine	Suspicious
Close	Spontaneous	Humorous
Shallow	Open	Cautious
Serious	Impulsive	Indifferent
Dependent	Cool	Cooperative
Calculating	Relaxed	Feminine
Warm	Evasive	Responsive
Tense	Silent	Dependent
Reserved	Self Assertive	
Frank	Informal	

Summarize and/or add values until you are satisfied that your expectations
have been expressed adequately:

_____
_____
_____

Part B. Hopes for Next Year

Another important part of your expectations set is what you want
to accomplish in the new culture--especially what hopes you have for the
first year there.

Career, study, and work goals are important, and so are personal,
life, and people goals (if they are different). The following experience
is designed to help you get in touch with what you'll be satisfied with
having done.

Find a comfortable spot (in the room) by yourself. One where
you can feel some privacy and can write notes. Relax and get
in touch with your breathing (then read on) . . . It's now
one year from the time you did the Cross-Cultural Workbook.
You're at a going-home party for yourself. You've just finished
a year in the new culture. Someone's talking about everything
that has happened during the year, mentioning past events,
jokes, and traumas. You drift off, daydreaming about everything
that's happened to you during the year and all the things you
feel best about having done or been involved with. Write those
things down:

_____
_____
_____

115

<u>Part C.</u>   Indicate by a flow line how you expect your next year to look
         after it is completed--specifically as influenced by being in a
         new culture.

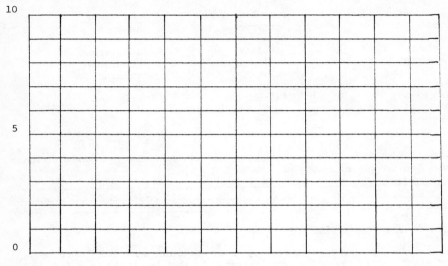

10

5

0

Mos.

Look over the time line chart you've drawn. What's going on during the
highs? What do you think will cause the lows? What will they be like?
What problems do you think you'll have?

_____
_____
_____

DEVELOPING A PLAN FOR ACTION

<u>Part A.   Goals</u>

        Many people feel more comfortable going into a new situation when
they have some plans or a structure thought out in advance--it gives them
something to tie their new experiences to, a way to organize their learnings, and a way to search for actions in a sometimes difficult and confusing time. During the course of this workbook you've touched on a lot
of experiences and feelings--both your own and the others in your group,
and you've looked at what you expect to find--including your expected
problems. But where do you want to be at the end of your first week?
the first month? the first half year? What, that you can't do now in the
new culture, would you like to be able to do then? What information do
you need? What skills do you want to develop?

116

Remembering that there are only so many hours in a day, look ahead and list your major goals for   the end of the first week, for the end of the first month, and for the end of the first half year:

_____

_____

_____

Part B.   Resources

Okay. Now you've got your goals and your expected problems. What resources do you have? As a group list,   all the resources that you can think of which can help you in any way. (Note: Hold off any discussion and criticism of items listed for at least ten minutes--just try to list as many things as possible, then after ten or so minutes discuss and evaluate them).

_____

_____

_____

Part C. Building your Plan

Now you have all the elements needed for developing a plan for what you can do to ease your learning of the new culture. This last step, however, is the one most often left out: deciding what to do first and then committing yourself to doing it. Take all the information you've been developing during the course of this workbook and decide what you are going to do to act on it. Develop some actions designed to meet your goals using some of your identified resources. Come up with five specific actions you <u>will</u> take <u>and</u> when you will take them.

Also, look ahead and see how you can use this material in the coming weeks. The concepts and information you've been touching on are not meant to just be forgotten--often people have reported that looking back at what they did in this workbook helped them focus in on their problems and find ways to deal with them months later. Some groups have found it especially useful to continue meeting from time to time to share their progress, and to give each other support and advice. Think about this and include it in your plans.

_____

_____

_____

RESPONDING TO A NEW CULTURE

So far you've been drawing on your own experiences and sharing them with the rest of the group. This is where most of the real learning takes place. Sometimes, however, it can help to examine the concepts and theories of people who have either studied or been through cross-cultural experiences to aid in crystallizing your learnings. The three short readings which follow contain some ideas which people who have had successful cross-cultural living experiences have pointed out to be important.

Our feeling is that they may help you to get a better picture of the experience you will be going through and will help you plan your strategy.

_____

_____

_____

A. Responses: Culture Shock

Everybody who enters and lives in a new culture for more than a month experiences culture shock. This means that the newcomer will experience feelings such as not belonging, alienation, unworthiness or inadequacy, and may lose touch with his or her own feelings. In many ways, the person will be experiencing real mental distress, but what must be recognized is that culture shock is a normative process. It is something that we all go through.

We do experience culture shock differently, however. Some people tend to get very depressed. This may mean that they withdraw from people of difference and have little energy to put forth in doing anything that is new or requires much effort. They feel victimized, and they look at others--particularly those in the new culture--as being the cause of their pain and torment.

Others may search desperately for similarities with their own culture or background and then try to rely upon these similarities for support. Those just out of a university environment may try to recreate some of the dominant qualities of that environment in their new situation. If they were heavily involved in sports, for example, they will try to get involved in similar activities in the new culture. If they previously relied a lot upon books, they will spend much of their time in the new culture simply reading. The tendency is to seek out something familiar from the past in an effort to dominate and exclude the present as well as to preserve one's own ego or sense of identity.

Old-timers say that culture shock can only be lived through, not dealt with. This does not seem to be true if you can just take the first step of recognizing that you are in culture shock. The whole thing is usually so deceptive--and we are so clever at inventing games to screen out reality--that we cannot or will not admit what we are going through.

If we can get through to our real feelings, the best thing to do is to face the reality and then deal with it. At this point we can acknowledge that we feel terrible (which is okey, because it is what everyone feels in a similar situation) and we can look for what actions we need to take to overcome these feelings. Action is terribly difficult for people in depression because they feel so ambivalent about things, but it is only action that will help. Action cuts through ambivalence and begins to resolve it.

An important question when you recognize that you are feeling down and lonely and all the rest is simply "What can I do to make myself feel good?" People in culture shock tend to be very puritanical and demanding of themselves--which only heightens the sense of discomfort and inadequacy. Answer the question of what would make you feel good and then go do it.

Feeling good as a person is the only way around culture shock and the only way into a new culture.

118

The following are some of the signs that may (they don't always) indicate that you are on the old culture shock trip.

Discuss these as a group, and think about the question of how much these may be signs of simple homesickness and how much they may indicate real culture shock.

* Yearning constantly for certain foods or personal comforts not readily available in the new culture.

* Escaping to maximum structure, minimum contact situations, such as movies or formal restaurants.

* Hanging around with fellow volunteers or others of your own ethnic group.

* Finding yourself talking about"them," and blaming "them" for all the problems you're having in your work or your personal adjustment.

* Finding yourself drinking excessively, or spending unusual amounts of time:

sleeping	playing cards (especially solitaire)
eating	reading when you should be doing
bathing	other things
grooming yourself	organizing or reorganizing your room,
daydreaming	equipment, etc.

*Or avoiding contact with people of the new culture in any of a hundred other ways which all boil down to one fact: You may be in culture shock, and you owe it to yourself as well as to those around you to start doing something about it.

B. Responses: Feedback and Overidentification

        Some things to keep in mind:

1. Feedback is the way we learn how well or how badly our actions are coming across to others.
2. Feedback is often very subtle. It is often only to our closest friends that we ever talk frankly about their actions and how we felt about them, and even then, usually our sharing of feelings is limited.
3. Feedback, both verbal and nonverbal, is cultural. It takes a long time to learn what it really means.
4. In a new culture, feedback systems may be widely different from what we're used to. At first, they may be totally unintelligible. What meant "you're doing fine" in your culture may mean "don't come any closer" in another culture.
5. When feedback is limited or confusing a common tactic is to mimic--to do what you see others doing--by picking up their actions and mannerisms.

119

6. Modelling is a basic form of learning, but it has to be in character with your other actions or it may appear ridiculous.
7. When carried to extremes it looks phony, and it is called overidentification. Examples would be to wear moccasins the first day on an Indian reservation, or talking ghetto talk when everybody knows you're from the white suburbs.
8. Overidentification can really turn people off. You're saying that you think you can fool them with this act, and that you're so clever that you can pick up in a day or so a personality or an identity that they've spent years putting together.
9. It's not real and they know it. You're not being yourself. Either the change to the new behavior was too sudden to be sincere, or even worse, you act differently when you're with "your own kind."
10. The only way out is to be yourself and find ways to be reinforced for it. Get to know someone who will tell you honestly how you're coming across in the new culture. If others from your own culture are available, help each other feed back on how you're doing in the new situation.
11. Be sensitive in the ways that people in the new culture give each other feedback. Then look at what they're telling you.

C. Responses: Maslow's Hierarchy of Needs

　　　　Attached is a brief description of Abraham Maslow's Need Hierarchy Model. This model is a very useful way to consider human motivation. Basically it states that a person cannot move up the hierarchy to more significant levels of need fulfillment until basic needs are satisfied. When they are not, the person shifts back down to satisfy those before other needs. For instance, you can't relate well to others if you are cold and hungry. This same model can be applied to a variety of other human situations, including learning to live in a new culture. People have to go through the basic levels of bodily maintenance, safety, familiarity and acceptance before approaching fluency in a new culture. Every group is different. Read the attached description of the need hierarchy, then as a group develop a need hierarchy describing the needs you expect to have as you try to adjust to a new culture. (What would be most important, second in importance, etc.)

THE MASLOW NEED HIERARCHY

　　　　Abraham Maslow theorized that experienced needs are the primary influences on an individual's behavior. When a particular need emerges, it determines the individual's behavior in terms of motivation, priorities, and action taken. Thus motivated behavior is the result of the tension-- either pleasant or unpleasant--experienced when a need presents itself. The goal of the behavior is the reduction of this tension or discomfort, and the behavior itself will be appropriate for facilitating the satisfaction of the need. Only unsatisfied needs are the prime sources of motivation.

　　　　Understanding behaviors and their goals involves insight into presently unsatisfied needs. Maslow developed a method for gaining insight by providing categories of needs in a hierarchical structure. He placed all human needs, from primitive or immature (in terms of the behavior they foster) to civilized or mature needs, in five need systems. He believed that there is a natural process whereby individuals fulfilled needs in ascending order from most immature to most mature. This progression through the need hierarchy is seen as the climbing of a ladder where the individual must have experienced secure footing on the first rung in order to experience the need to step up to the next higher rung. The awareness of the need to climb further up the ladder is a function of having fulfilled the need of managing the preceding rung, and only satisfactory fulfillment of this need will allow the individual to deal with the new need or rung. Inability to fulfill a lower-order need or difficulty in fulfilling a lower-order need may result in an individual's locking in on immature behavior patterns or may produce a tendency to return to immature behaviors under stress any time an individual feels a lower order need not fulfilled to his satisfaction. The individual may also revert to behaviors which fulfilled lower-order needs when the satisfaction of higher-order needs are temporarily blocked. That is not to say that any need is ever completely satisfied; rather, Maslow indicates that there must be at least partial fulfillment before an individual can become aware of the tensions manifested by a higher-order need and have the freedom to pursue its fulfillment.

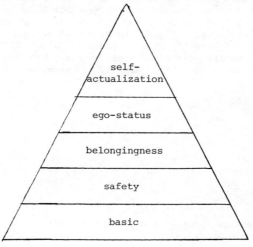

A HIERARCHY OF NEEDS, MASLOW

The Maslow Need Hierarchy is presented in the illustration above. The Basic level represents needs which reflect physiological and survival goals. At this level are such factors as shelter, clothing, food, sex, and other necessities. In a culture such as ours, where these basic needs are almost automatically met, there is not likely to be any need tension concerning the fulfillment of Basic needs. However, individuals adapt this Basic level upward to include such needs as avoidance of physical discomfort, pleasant working environment, or more money for providing creature comforts.

The second level of the hierarchy consists of the Safety needs. When an individual has at least partially fulfilled the Basic needs, he will experience the tensions relating to the needs of security, orderliness, protective rules, and general risk avoidance. These needs are often satisfied by an adequate salary, insurance policies, a good burglar alarm system for his business, a doorman for his apartment building, etc.

When Safety needs have been met, the individual will become less preoccupied with self and will endeavor to form interpersonal relationships. The relative success of this need for Belongingness will result in his feeling accepted and appreciated by others. Thus the third level needs concern family ties, friendship, and group membership.

When an individual feels secure in his relationships with others, he will probably seek to gain special status within the group. His need tension will be associated with ambition and a desire to excel. These Ego-status needs will motivate an individual to seek out opportunities to display his competence in an effort to gain social and professional awards.

Because Ego-status fulfillment is greatly dependent upon the ability of others to respond appropriately to the individual's efforts to perform in a superior way, they are the most difficult to fulfill satisfactorily. However, if the individual has gained satisfaction on level four, he may be able to move up to level five--Self-Actualization. At this level, the individual is concerned with personal growth and may fulfill this need by challenging himself to become more creative, demanding greater achievement of himself, and, in general, directing himself to measure up to his own criteria of personal success. Self-actualizing behaviors must include risk-taking, seeking autonomy, and developing freedom to act.

Reference: A. H. Maslow. Motivation and Personality, 2nd ed. (N.Y.: Harper and Row), 1970.

Excerpted from: Approaching Living in a New Culture: A Workbook for Cross-Cultural Learning, San Francisco, 1976. (with permission)

THE TRANS-CULTURAL STUDY GUIDE

edited by

Kenneth Darrow and Bradley Palmquist

LEARNING GOALS

1. A knowledge and understanding of the country in which one is living as a foreigner, including an appreciation of its recent historical experience.

2. A greater understanding of the process and problems of cross-cultural and international contact on both the personal level and the national level.

3. An appreciation of the way in which this country views the rest of the world, its international interests, and how these interests are perceived and reacted to by other nations.

4. An awareness of the overseas interests and activities of your own country, how these affect other peoples, and how these are perceived by other peoples.

5. A clearer understanding of foreign assistance programs, and the roles of foreigners as tourists, students, and commercial or service workers; how this foreign presence affects the host country; how these people and programs are viewed by both the 'hosts' and the 'visitors'; and the problems that arise from each of these.

6. A knowledge of the process and problems of development and rapid social change, and prospects for the future.

7. A first-hand experience with the difficulty of understanding a foreign culture in all its depth and diversity.

8. Greater empathy with a different people, and an enhanced ability to communicate with them.

123

9. A fuller awareness of oneself as a world citizen, of one's abilities, and of one's potential future roles; greater confidence, direction and commitment.

10. A new perspective on one's native land upon return from abroad.

METHODOLOGY

The following list of suggestions is designed to facilitate your work of finding, organizing, and recording data of various kinds. For the most part, these are very practical suggestions and not methodological theory or techniques. We feel, however, that for one who lacks field experience of any kind, even the simplest suggestions may prove to be helpful.

Finding Books and Printed Material

You will be able to take a few books with you which may be of use in your studies of the country; select these carefully. For the most part, however, you will have to find books there, and the libraries to which you are accustomed may be few and far between. We suggest the following:

1. There may be local libraries, especially those within the universities or colleges, which have useful books, especially about national history or current problems. Ask for permission to use such libraries and check them thoroughly soon after your arrival.

2. You will probably have several friends, especially older people such as professors, who have collections of books. Mention to them that you are looking for books on a particular subject and ask if they know where you might find them. If they have such books, they will probably not hesitate to loan them to you (assuming that you will return them promptly); if they don't, they may know someone who does. Also, your own students (if you are teaching) may have books you could borrow.

3. Local and national newspapers, some of which are in English, may be an invaluable source of information. Not only should you read them daily but also you should try to have a copy from which you can clip articles regularly. Clipping papers is much faster than making notes and will provide you with a great deal of data by the end of your stay. Articles should be carefully dated and could be organized according to topic by the numbers of the questions from this booklet. You may also want to attach comments or cross-references to an article. Clippings could be kept in folders or a small box.

4. There may be bookstores in the area which, if nothing else, may contain information booklets printed by the government. Browse through any such stores as soon as you have a chance.

5. Offices of government ministries or bureaus may have printed material available, such as census data, policy statements, regulations, or brochures. As long as the information is not at all sensitive and as long as you introduce and explain yourself and your interest thoroughly, you may be able to copy or borrow such material. Ask friends

124

for introductions into these government offices if possible. This
would be especially feasible for studies of public health or education.

Conversations and Interviews

It would obviously be a tragic loss of opportunity to spend most
of your time reading. Most of your knowledge about your setting will
come through your daily contacts with students and friends, and through
special trips or meetings. In many ways, you will employ the methodology of the ethnographer, who learns about a culture primarily as a parti-
cipant-observer and also through an in-depth knowledge of a few, carefully chosen persons (informants). Here are a few suggestions:

1. Always carry a pocket notebook with you. On any one day, you
can pick up many bits of information, usually through conversations, or
make new observations. You should make memory-jogging notes as soon as
possible so that you can later record and elaborate from these notes.
In order to make notes during a conversation without making anyone uncomfortable, you can, by explaining that you are trying to learn the
language, ask about and write down key words. (You should have a notebook for vocabulary anyway if you are trying to learn the language.)
Whether you try to make notes or not, during the course of particularly
interesting conversations, you should try to review the major points
and key words in your mind so that you can record brief notes later. At
the end of each day--and it is important to be regular--you can use these
brief notes or key words to record the information in your regular notebooks.

2. The classroom is, of course, one of the best opportunities for
learning about the society. As one of the most difficult problems in
the classroom is getting each student to talk at length and thus practice his English, it will be most helpful to the student and also interesting to you if you ask questions about topics of particular interest.
Certain subjects, especially politics and perhaps religious and other
social issues, may be taboo in the classroom, and you definitely should
not push into sensitive areas. However, especially if your students are
adults, it is most appropriate to ask about many aspects of the society,
including myths, history, and economics. Try collecting songs, tales,
and sayings. You may want to assign written compositions, or oral re-
ports, on particular topics which interest you. You may want to ask for
short autobiographical essays, which give you a sense of the historical
experience and personal motivations and world-views of your students.
But remember that your first responsibility is to teach, not to exploit
captive informants!

3. If you are especially interested in a particular area, for example
economics or education, it may be possible to arrange interviews with
knowledgeable people. These may be professors or administrators in
your school, or they may be government officials, to whom you could be
introduced by a friend. Let your interests be known, unless they are
likely to lead you into sensitive areas, and try to find out who can
help you. Try to seek out local intellectuals. During your stay, you
will surely meet many interesting people; you should try to arrange to
visit them again. Explain your interests, perhaps show them a list of
questions, and ask permission to make a few notes during your conversation.

4. You should try to establish several appropriate persons as your key informants. Depending on your interests, these may be the mothers in your neighborhood, a few of your students, the administrators in the university, the officials in the government office for economic development, members of student political groups, members of a particular religious group, local artists, and so on. It is better to be able to get to know and to question several people in depth than to converse with many persons briefly, for these purposes. A regular schedule of interviews might be set up. If you know that you will have a chance to talk with someone several times or more, you should try to plan your questions so that you will not offend or somehow alienate the person from the start by asking personal or very difficult questions. Remember that you are first a friend who should not use others for your own ends. Over time, as friendships develop, you will be able to ask questions and learn things which would not be possible initially.

5. There may be less organized and direct means for systematically questioning a particular social group; though you will not be able to make a sociological survey, you may have regular contact with members of some group in which you are interested. For example in Indonesia, each day you may ride in three or four different betjaks; you might use this opportunity to ask each driver several questions about where he was born, when he came to the city, how much he makes in a day, what kind of food he can buy for his family, etc. These questions do not require a great deal of language ability (though understanding the answers might) and could lead to a clearer understanding of many aspects of the local society (in this case, patterns of urbanization and under-employment).

6. It may be a particular advantage to find a friend who would serve as a translator on special occasions. He could accompany you to a special interview or such. Or he could help you translate particular articles from local newspapers. If you arrange for a tutor in the national language, he might help you with this translation.

Recording Data and Observations

You should keep a daily journal, which directly or indirectly attempts to answer and refer to the questions in the study guide. If you have special projects or areas of interest, you should keep separate notebooks for each. Notes from conversations, general observations, or other data should be recorded as soon as possible, preferably each evening. This may require a good deal of time. If it is possible that someone in your house or elsewhere might look through your notebooks and thus cause embarrassment or suspicion, it may be wise to substitute code names for people in your family or for political figures.

Periodically, perhaps every 1-3 months, you should write up a brief report on general observations and tentative conclusions about major issues. It is revealing to look back on these initial observations.

How Reliable is Your Information?

"One of the major dangers which any traveler faces in visiting another nation is the tendency to generalize on an inadequate number of

specific cases." (Experiment in International Living, Observation Guide.)
Beware the trap of automatically assuming that because you are given a
particular answer to a question, that that is the correct answer, or
that the particular informant even thinks it is the correct answer.
Often people, trying to be helpful, would rather give any answer than
to tell you that they really don't know. Especially unreliable is any
hypothesis or analysis that you yourself have proposed, and to which
you have simply received an affirmative reply. Beware of people telling
you what they think you want to hear. Ask around, check it out with
others who may have a similar perspective, and see if you get the same
answer.

AREAS FOR TRANS-CULTURAL STUDY

The Transcultural Study Guide breaks useful cross-cultural knowledge into twelve areas: Economics, Politics, Social Structure, Roles
of Women and Men, Religion and Beliefs, Music and Art, Food, Education,
Communications, Health and Welfare, The Trans-Cultural Experience, Development. Here are some representative examples of the kinds of questions suggested:

Society and the Individual: City, Town, or Village

The heading for this section suggests a particular perspective
for study, that is, society and social structure as they affect the
single individual. However, one would not feel restricted to this if
the resources are available for undertaking a study from a different
perspective. Remember that in most of the world, much decision-making
and other activities take place on the level of small groups, rather
than the level of the individual.

1.a. What are the occupational groups in your locality? What are
the income levels of the groups? How does occupation and income relate to housing patterns? Which are the choice residential areas of
the community? Which areas are overcrowded? How do occupation and
income relate to social groupings (friends, people one would see off
the job, etc.)?
    b. Do villages as units have particular economic activities/
specializations?
2. What is the educational level of different class or status
groups? What are the educational expectations of children of families within those groups? Is the quality, type, and level of education an individual receives related to his ethnic, cultural, or re-
liguous background? Does the educational system operate to inten-
sify or mediate the status and class divisions within the society?
Are educated people simply absorbed into the upper classes, thereby
cutting off connections with their former peers?
3. Level of political activity: What do people classify as political activities? What percentage of each class or social group
can be expected to engage in political activities? How often? Are
there elections? What groups of people vote? What political groups
or candidates are associated with what social or class groups?

4. Associations: These can be formal or informal, and are often multifunctional (e.g., an Islamic social welfare organization). What kinds of organizations are most common? Most prestigious? Most influential? Most active? What kinds of people (age, sex, economic class, educational level) compose the memberships of these associations? Are there existing rivalries between different organizations? Do such rivalries appear to be productive or destructive? What are some of the latent functions of these associations?

5. Recreation: What are the important leisure time activities? For adults? For children? What is the relative importance of TV, radio, movies, card-playing, relaxed conversation, outdoor sports (participation and observation), informal visits, musical and dramatic events, etc.? Which population groups participate most heavily in each of these? How does the local concept of leisure compare with your own?

6. Is there much movement in and out of the city of individuals? Of groups? How are new members of the community viewed?

Family and the Individual

This area will probably afford the greatest possibilities for learning and study but will also require the greatest amount of tact and sensitivity. Be aware of male and female role-differentiation and aspects and problems of child-rearing.

1. What is the average size of families? Is this increasing or decreasing? What is the average household size? Does the household include grandparents? Aunts, uncles, and their children? Others?

2. Is there a national family planning program? How old is the program? How successful is it? Which characteristics of the culture seem to act as barriers to family planning? Which ones facilitate it? Describe the various approaches that the family planning workers are using. Are there economic reasons behind resistance to family planning (e.g., more hands in the fields, security in old age if more children survive, etc.)? (See Family Planning under HEALTH.)

3. What are the social relationships within households and families? Who is the head of the household? What is the role of women within the household? Male children? Female children? The aged? How are decisions which affect the entire family made? Who handles economic matters dealing with the family or household? Who controls the rearing and socialization of children? What are the priorities of a family (e.g., number of children, income, material possessions, kind of housing, social status, or physical well-being)?

4. What constitutes a good husband, wife, son, daughter? How much independence do young people have? At what age are they considered adults?

5. At what age do children marry? How do marriages come about? Who arranges and/or pays for a wedding ceremony? Are they costly? What roles do parents play in selecting spouses for their children? Do newly married couples form new households? What is the expectation or possibility that children will move away from the area in which they were raised, after marriage? What relationship do two married people have with their parents?

128

6. What is the frequency of divorce? What government and religious regulations affect a divorce? What rights do women have under these regulations?

7. The average family in the U.S. remains in one household for a period of 3-4 years. In this country?

8. Are there helpers or servants? Are they generally relatives? How are they regarded and treated? What seems to be the nature of their social, economic, and personal relationships with those for whom they work?

9. What are the important social customs of the society? Describe table manners, forms of greeting and their social significance, manners and customs between men and women, expressions of deference and respect, etc. What are the origins and meanings of these customs? How do they relate to class or role differentiation?

Personal Awareness and Growth

1. Albert Camus writes: "Your successes and happiness are forgiven you only if you generously consent to share them. But to be happy it is essential not to be too concerned with others. Consequently, there is no escape. Happy and judged, or absolved and wretched."

   If you have been confronted with a very impoverished situation and witnessed more suffering than ever before in your life, have you had this sense that your own happiness is incompatible with a deep concern for others? How can you deal with it? To what extent does guilt influence or motivate you?

2. Levi-Strauss writes: "Why does he (the anthropologist) decide to disdain (his own society), reserving for societies distant and different from his own the patience and devotion which he has deliberately withheld from his fellow-citizens? . . . At home the anthropologist may be a natural subversive, a convinced opponent of traditional usage; but no sooner has he in focus a society different from his own than he becomes respectful of even the most conservative practices."

   Have you found that at times, out of a desire to be respectful of your host culture, you have been unnaturally conservative about social forms? If you are in some ways an advocate of a counter-culture in your own country, do you see any inconsistency between your actions here and there? If so, why do you think this is true? Should you be more tolerant and patient with your own society? On the other hand, societies are living, changing entities. They depend upon the actions and thinking of their members for energy and new directions. Would you agree that behavior differing radically from social norms is acceptable for a native of a particular society? Would the same behavior on the part of a foreigner be unacceptable? Discuss.

3. Have you found a lack of the kind of intellectual orientation and discussion which you are familiar with in a university environment? Why? Would this happen at home if you were away from the university? What concerns occupy the local people--meditation, art, complicated games, other? If you have experienced intellectual and/or emotional

solitude, have you been able to use this to work within yourself? In what ways?

4. To what extent have you found yourself to be self-directed and self-motivated intellectually? In all your other activities? How would you compare your present work and its vitality with that which you usually experience within the university?

5. Do you feel that thoroughgoing communication with your local friends is very difficult, because you don't have similar life experiences? What new modes of communication have you developed?

6. In what ways are your personal habits of consumption and spending changing? Do you find yourself more meticulous about your possessions and more thrifty with your momey? Why? How do you think this will affect you when you return to your native country? Why? If you don't think the two are related, why not?

7. How have your thoughts about further academic work and potential career been influenced by your experience in this country?

8. What has your experience told you about the notion of boundaries of race, culture, and nation among peoples of the world? How has your ability to penetrate another society and culture affected the above? Is the term boundaries appropriate? What would be a better term?

9. In terms of reinterpreting and modifying your life-style, do you think that you have adopted many practices and ideas from the culture you are in? What kinds?

10. In what ways have you found yourself to be clearly a product of your own culture in your habits, orientations, expectations, motives, and mind-frame? What specific aspects of yourself are cultural baggage, and which are essential to your personal identity (e.g., whereas a lack of concern about time and punctuality may cause trouble for you in our culture, in others it may be expected and reinforced)? To what extent can you conform to local values and expectations and still be yourself? Consider your social behavior, personal experience, mannerisms, and habits in the cross-cultural setting.

11. What is necessary for you to be happy and fulfilled in your everyday life? To what extent may these needs be met in the new cultural setting (e.g., privacy, intimate companionship, honest feedback, intellectual stimulation/communication of a particular kind, certain favorite foods)? Do you think you will find yourself caught between two cultures? How do you think your experience will make it difficult to live in your native country?

12. Culture shock has been defined as the need for something familiar and excessive irritation from minor frustrations. Describe this phenomenon in relation to your own experience. What differences seem most noticeable initially? After a period of time in your new environment? How would you define culture shock?

Interactions

1. Cultural fatigue has been defined as the lack of energy or emotional projection for social relations. Discuss this in relation to your own experiences, pointing out possible ways to resolve the problem of cultural fatigue.

2. Describe your experiences of miscommunication when talking or making plans with local people (e.g., perhaps when your friend says "yes" he actually means "maybe," and when he says "maybe," he is trying to imply "no."

3. Body language provides cues in situations where thoughts and feelings are not expressed verbally. However, there is much room for misunderstanding this type of communication in cross-cultural relations. Consider the example of relations with the opposite sex, where eye contact, a smile, and hand-holding may communicate something entirely different from what you are accustomed to. Consider how non-verbal communication operates to express the following: romantic interest, anger in varying degrees (withdrawal, violence, or excessive politeness?), impatience, boredom, sadness, happiness, maturity, authority, respect, and shame.

4. Consider your role in the community, as a teacher or student, and as a foreigner representing certain values and ideals. What influence might these have on the local people?

5. What do the local people think are the most salient characteristics of your own culture? This may lead to some additional insight into their self-image as well.

6. What impact has the local community and the teaching or studying experience had on your own values, ideals, and views of the world.

Sense of Humor

1. What kinds of humor are acceptable? What forms do they take? Are practical jokes common?
2. Are there any topical areas that are taboo or given special emphasis (e.g., government activity, sex, corruption)?
3. What seem to be the elements of a good joke?
4. What kinds of jokes are told about foreigners?
5. Do these people commonly laugh at themselves? Are they inclined to laugh at their difficulties?
6. Is odd behavior met with ridicule or amusement?
7. Do the people find foreign accents or ways amusing?
8. What kind of humor predominates in films? TV? Radio?
9. Are jokes ever shared between individuals of different status? Is a person likely to tell a joke to a superior?

Excerpted from The Trans-Cultural Study Guide, 1975, Volunteers in Asia, Box 4543, Stanford, California 64305 (with permission).

CHAPTER VII

CRITICAL INCIDENTS

CRITICAL INCIDENTS EXERCISE

Paula Barnak

Description

Critical Incidents present situations or encounters involving
an attitude or cultural value critical to one's understanding of or
performance with a specific non-American culture. The incidents are
open-ended; that is, there is no right answer to be guessed or learned.
Rather, as interactions between two people in a given situation, the
incidents should be seen as having several possible explanations and
solutions depending on the personality and style of the viewer.

Purpose

The Critical Incidents Exercise has several uses. One, it can
be used simply to initiate a general discussion and to create interest
in the understanding of American as well as non-American culture.
Secondly, it can be used in conjunction with and based upon any non-
American culture experience in order to increase sensitivity to cultural differences. Thirdly, with a prepared scale and questions, it
can be used individually and/or in small groups to stimulate open discussion, thus allowing the trainer and trainees to explore together
their responses, attitudes, and value judgments.

This exercise can be used effectively to accomplish to facilitate
the following more specific objectives:

• To introduce the trainee to additional aspects of a non-American
  culture.

• To introduce the trainee to the trainer's role and the kinds of
  problems he may encounter.

• To expose the trainee to a variety of approaches that may be
  taken (as he becomes aware of the diversity of opinions, attitudes, and ideas that exist in his group).

• To force the trainee to work through the different views of his
  group--to agree or agree to disagree, but with an understanding
  of the different positions and the possible consequences of
  various actions.

• To involve the trainee in a decision (problem)-solving process by which he begins to see how people respond depending upon the cultural values they hold.

Development

Content for Critical Incidents should be gathered from the experiences of personnel in their day-to-day interactions with the non-American participants. In developing Critical Incidents, refer to the following guidelines:

1. The situation or incident should represent an area of <u>conflict</u> of cultures, values, standards, or goals.
2. The situation should be one where the solution is not obviously apparent, <u>or</u> one where there might be considerable <u>controversy</u> regarding the most appropriate or effective action to be taken --depending on one's background and/or philosophy.
3. The situation should include the <u>conditions</u> under which the situation occurred and the action was taken.
4. The situation should be written in concise language.

Format

The following example is taken from a Critical Incidents Exercise included in another training program.

Critical Incident

Yesterday I gave a test to the Saudi Recruits at my station. The test reviewed all the steps we have covered so far. Two of the Saudis did very poorly; in fact, one failed completely. When I began to discuss the tests results with them, they simply shrugged their shoulders and said, "In shallah" (If God wills). So I said, "But God didn't answer the test. You did."

* * * *

How do you feel about the way this situation was handled? To what extent do you agree or disagree with what was done or said? Rate your response on the scale below by circling the appropriate number.

1	2	3	4	5
Completely agree				Completely disagree

What Saudi cultural value (if any) is reflected here?
What American cultural value (if any) is reflected here?
How would <u>you</u> have handled this situation?
What could you have done to prevent this situation from arising in the first place?

134

Procedure

The following procedures pertain to using this exercise with the prepared rating scale and questions. The purpose of the scale is to help the trainee focus his thinking and, in the case of small group work, to make it easier for them to arrive at a point of departure for discussion.

Individual Work

1. Hand out package of Critical Incidents to each participant.

2. Review the instruction:

   • Read the incident.
   • Indicate on the scale the extent to which you agree (Why?) or disagree (Why?) with the action taken.
   • Determine the cultural values involved.
   • Determine what you would have done in the situation.

3. Given a package of 10-15 incidents, allow participants 20-30 minutes for individual work.

Small Group Work

1. If small group discussion is to follow the individual work before the summary session, divide the group into subgroups of 3 or 4 participants each.

2. Review the instructions:

   • Discuss your attitudes/responses/solutions for each incident.
   • Choose someone as group recorder to write down your group response/solution to be shared in the summary session.

3. Depending on the time available, the small groups should work through all the incidents or those selected in advance as most pertinent.

4. Circulate from group to group. The facilitator should not interject his own opinions, but take note of the attitudes coming out and reasons offered for various actions. Do try to focus the trainees' attention on the situation at hand, however, if they wander off the track.

Summary in Group Assembly

1. Ask all the groups to assemble. Again, given the time constraints, select the particular incidents to be discussed.

2. Ask each group representative what cultural values were involved and what his group decided as an appropriate response or solution. Writing each response on a flip chart will make discussion easier.

3. Discuss each in turn. Focus on the cultural values involved and whether or not the action taken, or suggested alternatives, took these values into consideration. Discuss the possible ramifications of each solution suggested.

4. It is not necessary to reach group consensus, but it may be pointed out that one action is perhaps more appropriate in a given situation than another.

5. Some of the participants may complain that the situation is not explained in sufficient detail, or that they did not have time enough to make their decisions. This is a good opportunity to suggest that they may never know _everything_ about an individual situation, particularly what other Nationals are thinking, and that they may have to make many decisions with little time to reflect or to collect information.

Excerpted with permission from: Iceland Defense Force (IDF) Overseas Diplomacy Program, Vol. II, "Overseas Diplomacy Training Program Manual." Center for Research and Education, Denver, Colorado, May 1976.

CRITICAL INCIDENTS

Making Value Judgments and Reaching Consensus

Henry Holmes and Stephen Guild

Introduction

This is a paper-and-pencil technique which gives participants a
chance to examine particular incidents (each one chosen for its importance to understanding a critical cultural problem) and make value
judgments about them. It also requires, as a second step, that they
move from this position of individual judgment to a consensus with
other members of a group, a process whereby they come to understand
some of the problems and benefits involved in reaching compromise.
Critical incidents can be useful in illustrating day-to-day cultural
problems, particularly ones concerned with cultural change. Leaders
are encouraged to develop incidents from their own experience.

Procedure

Each critical incident is a short (5-10 lines) account of a cultural event, whose outome has cross-cultural significance. Between
10 and 20 of these incidents are presented to participants, along with
an answer sheet.
The answer sheet is a "forced choice" technique whereby participants must make a judgment on the action which the incident describes.
The sheet gives a scale of "Completely agree" (1) to "Completely disagree" (9) for each action described, and space for a brief justifica-
tion of the rating. The leader emphasizes that there are no "right"
answers to any of the incidents.
Each participant responds individually on paper to each incident.
Then all are brought together in groups of four or five, and asked to:

(1) arrive at a group consensus rating,
(2) give a mutually agreeable reason for the rating, and
(3) an acceptable substitute action in the incident.

Voting or averaging is not allowed; a true consensus is the aim.

Critical Incidents

1. Juan had been recently assigned to live in a remote district and
   carry out a health survey. Because he was friendly and had been

educated in the city, village people often came to his house to visit in the evening, some of them staying quite late. Juan, however, was accustomed in the city to having time to himself. Also his treks to other villages made him tired, so these late visits became a burden. On this particular night, exhausted, he finally tells them, "Excuse me please, 'Uncles,' but I am tired and have to sleep now."

2. Kumar works in a mill managed by a European. Recently he has been late getting to work in the afternoon and has been scolded by his boss. Today, having finished lunch he realizes he had better walk quickly, for fear of being late to the mill again.

   As he approaches the mill, he sees Indru, a man from his home village and one of his best friends, coming along toward him. Indru is just visiting from the village and has time for a chat and a drink, something Kumar would ordinarily (in their own village) welcome as a matter of course, whatever the time of day. Now, however, as they exchange greetings, Kumar breaks off the conversation politely but abruptly and hurries off to work.

3. My father was in important chief in our province during the colonial period, so I used to accompany him to important functions. One of these was the coronation of our Sultan. When the Sultan entered the great hall everyone else stood; but the British officials quickly sat down. I was shocked; it reminded me how our roles are mainly for show, while they have all the power.

   I am a mature civil servant now, and have been able to send my three oldest children to England to study.

4. Mindo was a new teacher in this Southeast Asian village. The school yard needed improvement and Mindo knew that the students could fix things up if they were properly organized to do it. Ordinarily, manual labor was not done by educated people but the school couldn't afford to hire laborers. Mindo found, though, that the students almost enjoyed the work if they could do it in large groups. Eventually the job was nearly done and Mindo, who liked to encourage independence, assigned particular individuals to separate areas of the school. One of them, assigned to dig a trench near the edge of the school yard, refused to work and asked to go home. Mindo was angry and perplexed.

5. I am president of the local school association, in a district whose residents are mostly poor and members (like me) of a minority group. Many of these people want our school to have teachers from the same minority group, because they are afraid our culture will be overcome by the ways of the majority. The city education officials who administer our district insist that it is they who must select teachers for us, for fear that the quality of education will fall. I have decided to accept this view, because good education is the hope of our people.

6. After going to school abroad for five years, Sutira returned to her country, where her large extended family lived in the capital city.

138

When Sutira told her father that she wanted to find an apartment with a friend in another part of the city, he was troubled. He had plenty of room here, and besides she was part of the family. Her education was a thing of prestige to the family. Sutira felt she wanted her own life, however, and proceeded to find a new place, even though it cost her much of her savings.

7. As I do my work I do my best to introduce in local villagers the idea of freedom and democracy. Most rural people are locked into an age-old authoritarian system; I think I can show them a better way. Constantly I look for local leaders who see things as I do, so together we can work to change the system.

8. Mr. Subramaniam is a senior Indian Government Official, who was attending a conference in a European capital. Lonely one evening at the hotel, he saw a European seated nearby in the lounge and struck up a conversation.

The man, a Mr. West, was unfamiliar with India but was nonetheless amiable and expressed interest in Mr. Subramaniam. During the conversation, a friend of Mr. West's passed by. Mr. West introduced Mr. Norton (which was the friend's name) to Mr. Subramaniam, and Mr. Norton said how glad he was to meet Mr. Subramaniam, and so on. Shortly, Mr. Norton asked Mr. West if he could have dinner with him the following evening. Mr. West accepted enthusiastically. Neither man asked Mr. Subramaniam, who was right there, if he would like to go.

Mr. Subramaniam, feeling unwanted and ashamed, asked to be excused and left immediately.

9. Jeanne was a teacher in a rural area overseas. One of her students, whose father was an influential political leader, had done little work during the term. Jeanne had felt obliged to turn in a failing grade for her. The headmaster called Jeanne in and asked her to reconsider the failing grade. She refused.

10. I had been working to set up a day care center in the community. Though I had worked hard, support from community members was slow in coming. The need for the day care center was so great, I decided to seek help from a large philanthropic organization, located in the provincial capital. This effort worked, and the center was completed promptly.

For each incident, select your reaction from the following scale, then answer the other questions. The number you select should indicate the extent to which you agree with the opinions, attitudes, or actions of the person(s) described in each incident.

1. Completely disagree
2. Almost completely disagree
3. Disagree quite a bit
4. Disagree more than agree
5. Neutral
6. Agree more than disagree
7. Agree quite a bit
8. Almost completely agree
9. Completely agree

---

1. Rating_____   What would you do?
    Why?

2. Rating_____   What would you do?
    Why?

3. Rating_____   What would you do?
    Why?

4. Rating_____   What would you do?
    Why?

5. Rating_____   What would you do?
    Why?

6. Rating_____   What would you do?
    Why?

7. Rating_____   What would you do?
    Why?

8. Rating_____   What would you do?
    Why?

9. Rating_____   What would you do?
    Why?

10. Rating_____   What would you do?
    Why?

Reprinted with permission from Henry Holmes and Stephen Guild, _Manual of Teaching Techniques for Intercultural Education_, University of Massachusetts, Amherst, 1971.

CHAPTER VIII

CASE STUDIES

THE CASE STUDY METHOD

Robert Ross

Briefly, case studies are analogues of actual situations written
as close to reality as possible. The advantage of the case study
lies not within the described case, in which there may be more or less
descriptive material than the individual or group might like to have,
but in the almost unlimited potential for thinking about, talking about
and deciding about the many ways of solving the problem, discussing the
human and organizational interactions described, and analyzing both
organizational and human successes and failures. Good case studies
are neither a base for entertainment, nor an opportunity for nostalgia,
"boy, does that sound familiar, I remember,..." etc.. Case studies
open up the opportunity for novice and "old hand," to think carefully,
analytically, and understandingly about the experiences that the cases
describe. None of the situations set forth in the cases is simple or
capable of easy solution; many of the situations depend upon the
attitudes, the sentiments, and the prejudices of the people involved
rather than upon the actual events. Hence,these cases engender the
need for careful thought: first, about one's own personal reactions
to the situation and the people coping with it; second, about the
points of view of each of the characters involved; and finally,
about the possible outcomes of such situations and their effects upon
the various protagonists. In other words, the case studies are designed
to develop a method of approaching situations that will facilitate
maximum understanding of those situations, of the people in them, and
of the several outcomes that might result when one or another of the
people emphasizes certain values rather than others. Furthermore,
the case studies afford the student an opportunity to practice this
method of tackling problems before he is personally involved in situations
that he may find confusing, frightening, or overwhelming." (Barry, et al,
p.10)
        To think carefully, analytically and understandingly as mentioned
above is not as easy as it seems. In using case studies, seemingly
simple situations when analyzed carefully are in reality complex,
open-ended situations which may be resolved only over a long span of
time. Analyzing the presently described case in terms of precedents
(how the organization getsto what is described) personalities, programs,
solutions, goals, remediation, intervention, consultation and even
an "organizational funeral," can lead the group to multiple, even
contrary, suggestions and the group analyzing the case may suddenly find
that it is no longer concentrating on the case study, but on its own
problems of coming to consensus about proposing solutions. Especially

142

will this be so if the group is mandated to report back, in a time-frame, proposed solutions in the case studies they are examining.

What then is the case method?

1. It is a description of a specific situation,   near to reality as analogy permits (with names changed to protect the innocent).
2. The focus is on experience, therefore an actual situation where action/decisions can be made.
3. Thus the discussion centers in an actual, multi-faceted situation.
4. Case studies emphasize the particular rather than the general as much as possible.
5. The participants are to feel that they have had the experience that the case study describes.
6. Therefore the case study must be of interest so the participant can "get into it."
7. The reader/individual or the reader/group do the decision-making. There are no observers or spectators in the group.
8. The decision-making process itself can be dissected and analyzed as the group moves toward solutions.
9. Ideally, the case study method, when used well, gets the participant in the habit of making decisions.
10. If a time-frame is established, i.e. 60 minutes, 2 hours, etc., decision-making includes use of time. We have to decide, and as the saying has it, "not to decide is to decide."
11. To make good decisions, all the factual material in the case study should be used.
12. Case studies are best when they come as close to reality as possible; therefore, they should reflect day-to-day and run-of-the-mill decision-making with opportunity for differences of opinion. Resolving those differences of opinion into consensus, or majority-minority decisions is part of the task, (the difference between unity and unanimity).

CASE STUDY

Henry Holmes and Stephen Guild

General Description. The case study is similar to the critical
incident but is much more extensive and detailed. Where the critical
incident highlights a situation, the case study explores it in depth.
The case study is more like a story, with chapters, than one vignette.
As with critical incidents, discussion is an important part of the
case study method where the students can express their opinions and
explore different values and attitudes.

Case studies are extended explorations of a particular situation.
They can range from several to many pages and may become very complex,
with many different characters and points of view. They may or may not
demand a decision or resolution at the end. There are some sources of
case study material but they may also be constructed from one's own
experiences or from the experiences of others who have been abroad, e.g.,
foreign students, returned Peace Corps volunteers, businessmen, etc.

Group Size. As with critical incidents, case studies can be used
with a normal class size; but they work better in smaller groups,
where students can participate more in the discussion--ten to twelve
students would be ideal.

Time Required. Normally, a set of case studies would be used
over a long period of time--several weeks perhaps. A single case
study could be the basis for one class period or could extend longer,
depending upon the class and the case study material.

Materials Utilized. Case Study Material.

Physical Setting. Any standard classroom. Moveable chairs are
highly desirable, especially if the group is broken into small groups.
If it is a large single group, arranging the room in a single circle
is important for the discussion.

Process. 1. The written case studies should be handed out to the
students, and after they have had time to read and think about the
particular one appropriate for this class, the teacher should begin
by asking for different opinions on the case and the resolution.

144

2. The teacher may want to step out of the role of discussion leader once the conversation gets started. He or she may want to remain only as a clarifier, or if the discussion lags, as an initiator of a different point of view.

3. When it seems as if the discussion has come to a satisfactory ending point, or even before that time in some cases, the teacher should summarize the discussion and the major points. As with the critical incidents, there are no "right" answers and students should understand this.

4. At this time you may want to proceed to another case, or you may want to relate the discussion to other parts of the lesson or unit.

Special Instructions. In many instances case studies are gathered in a single booklet around a central theme. However, they may also be solitary cases which fit into other materials.
To write case studies will require some extra effort, but it will pay off in the reality a case study brings to discussion. When developing your own, you should keep in mind the points listed under this heading in the "Critical Incident" section.

Resources.

Wright, Albert R. and Mary Anne Nammons. Guidelines for Peace Corps Cross-Cultural Training. Estes Park, Colorado: Center for Research and Education: or Washington, D.C., Peace Corps Office of Training Support, 1970.

Spicer, Edward, ed. Human Problems in Technological Change. New York: Russell Sage Foundation, 1952.

Niehoff, Arthur. A Casebook of Social Change. Chicago: Aldine Publishing Co., 1966.

Examples: 1. The frail, old, almost totally blind lady appeared at every clinic session and sat on the dirt floor enjoying the activity. She was dirty and dishevelled, and obviously had very little, even by Malaysian kampong (local village) standards.
One day the visiting nurse happened upon this woman in her kampong. She lived by herself in a rundown shack about 10 by 10 feet. When questioned how she obtained her food, she said she was often hungry, as she only received food when she worked for others -- pounding rice, looking after the children, and the like.
The nurse sought to obtain help for the woman. It was finally resolved that she would receive a small pension from the Department of Welfare which would be ample for her needs.

At each weekly clinic, the woman continued to appear. She had
become the center of attention, laughed and joked freely, and obviously
enjoyed her increased prestige. No change was noted in her physical
status, however. She continued to wear the same dirty black dress
and looked no better fed.

The nurse asked one of the rural health nurses to find out if the
woman needed help in getting to a shop to buy the goods she seemed
so sorely in need of.

In squatting near the woman, the rural health nurse noted a wad
of bills in the woman's basket. "Wah," she said, "It is all here.
You have spent nothing. Why is that?"

The woman laughed and then explained: "I am saving it all for my
funeral."

Discussion Guide.

How do people approach activity?

What are the important goals in life?

What is the nature of social reciprocity?

What is the attitude toward problem-solving?

What is the nature of property?

What are the relationships between man and nature?

What personal qualities are valued?

What are the attitudes toward change?

2. During a busy clinic session, a mother brought a girl about
four years old to the nurse. Upon examination, it was found that the
child had a fever of 103° F., and had been suffering from diarrhea for
three days. When questioned, the mother said that the child had been
unable to take rice for "some time".

The mother was advised that medication at the clinic would not
suffice. She must bring the child to the hospital for consultation.
She was advised that she and the child could go to the hospital that
day in the medical vehicle. However, because she had other children
at home, the mother said she would first go home and arrange for their
care and go to the hospital later.

The following day, when the nurse checked the hospital, the child
was not there. When she asked the hospital attendant about the case,
he answered that the mother had brought the child to the dispensary,
but because she had screamed and become hysterical, he had sent them
home.

146

As soon as she could, the nurse traced the child to her village, and discussed the matter further with the mother. During the conversation, it was learned that the child's older brother had had similar symptoms about two weeks previously. It was mentioned by the child's grandmother that another child in the family had died two years before in the district hospital of "fever". The nurse re-examined the child and found the temperature now to be 104° F. She explained to the mother and grandmother the danger of convulsions and further complications and then personally sponged the child. Finally the mother agreed to take the child back to the hospital but the child refused. Therefore, nothing could be done. The nurse decided that she would return to the clinic, get the medical vehicle and personally take the child directly to the hospital.

That afternoon the nurse returned to the village with the vehicle. She proceeded directly to the house and found several neighbors and older women sitting on the floor near the child. Some betel nuts, a bottle and a small burning lamp were on the floor near the child. The child appeared to be resting quietly on her mat. The usual greetings were exchanged and the nurse took her place on the floor near the mother. Shortly she was offered some coffee.

The nurse then suggested that they prepare to go to the hospital. The mother watched quietly as the nurse went to pick up the child who now appeared asleep on the mat. The grandmother then stated that it was not necessary to take the child to the hospital since she was no longer ill. The women sitting near the child nodded their heads in agreement.

The nurse examined the child and found her temperature now to be 101° F. The child roused at that point and the grandmother proceeded to feed her a bottle of water which the child took, along with a banana. The grandmother commented that there was no need to send the child to the hospital since the Tok Bomoh (traditional medicine man) "had taken care of it". The mother nodded agreement and the conversation turned to something else. Shortly thereafter the nurse drove back to the clinic.

The following day she again returned to the child's home. The child was up and about, and eating small amounts of rice. Although the child appreared to be recovering, the nurse was convinced that a relapse would occur unless preventive actions were taken. Despite her efforts to convince the mother that continued treatment was necessary, the response was always the same: "Tok Bomoh has taken care of it." The nurse tried several times to explain why it was impossible for the Bomoh's treatment to be effective, and that although the child looked well, it might actually be sick. Finally, the nurse became adamant in her concern and demanded that the child be sent to the hospital for "proper" treatment. To this the grandmother replied: "Proper treatment has already taken one child from us." Insulted, the nurse left.

The next time the nurse visited the village, she was approached by the village chief before making her rounds. He assured her that everyone was well, and that her services were not required, saying: "I'm sure that nurse has better things to do."

Discussion Guide.

What different attitudes toward health and healing are demonstrated here?

What are the differences perceived between a hospital nurse and a village spirit doctor?

How are decisions made in different societies? What constitutes authority?

What different attitudes toward child rearing are suggested here?

What relationships are perceived between man and nature?

Excerpted from: A Manual of Teaching Techniques for Intercultural Education, University of Massachusetts, Amherst, 1971. (with permission)

148

CHAPTER IX

OTHER GROUP EXERCISES

GROUP DISCUSSION
Paula Barnak

Description

A group discussion, centered on a specific topic, problem, or question, can be an effective way for people to learn. It is an interchange of ideas among the members of a group, however, and not a question/answer dialogue between the discussion leader and members of the group.

The leader's role is to: (1) insure that all members of the group are encouraged to participate; (2) keep those who talk too much from monopolizing the conversation; (3) keep the discussion focused on the topic and moving logically toward the goal; (4) clarify statements; (5) restate and challenge ideas; and (6) summarize main point.

Purpose

A group discussion is most effective when one or more of the following conditions exist:

- There is prior experience or knowledge of the subject on the part of the participants.

- There is a need (goal) to create new ideas, actions, and responses from these experiences.

- There are learning and action situations in which decisions and judgments are difficult.

- There is a need for airing of personal values, attitudes, and involvement.

- There is a need to determine participants' expectations of the training program (needs analysis).

The following objectives can be accomplished and/or facilitated by using a group discussion:

- Provide a means by which trainees can understand a complicated topic.

- Focus on trainees' previous experience, relating it to new ideas and situations.

- Force trainees to formulate and present their views.

- Force trainees to justify and defend their views.

Procedure

Often the leader must prepare or bring into play key questions to make sure that the topic is adequately covered and that the critical points are brought out.

Different kinds of questions invite different kinds of responses. For instance, a question with a "correct" answer serves the purpose of establishing data, but does not encourage people to open up and contribute their own thoughts and ideas. Many discussion leaders, therefore, like to start the ball rolling with an open-ended question, one

150

which requires thinking rather than a yes or no answer. Such questions have no "right" or "wrong" answer and thus encourage participants to say what they think. Examples: What came to your mind as you watched...? How did you feel about...? In what ways did...? What did you like about...?

Focusing questions are used when specific points need to be brought out. Examples: What happened when...? What implications can be drawn from...? What are some of the reasons for the differences between...?

Probing questions may be required if a contribution seems irrelevant or unclear. Examples: Would you give us an example? Would you elaborate on that a bit?

Prompting questions may have to be directed toward those who are not participating. Examples: What do you think about that, Bob? Bill, what has been your experience?

Summarizing questions are used when you want to elicit a review of the information the group has shared. Examples: In what ways did ...happen? What are the major factors in...?

Here are some techniques for asking questions and guiding a discussion which may be helpful:

- Phrase questions so that a "discussing" answer, rather than yes or no, is required. Yes or no questions, however, may be useful to draw timid persons into the discussion.

- Phrase questions impartially so that they are not "leading" questions.

- If no one offers to answer a question, rephrase it.

- Accept each contribution as worthy of consideration.

- If a contribution seems irrelevant, ask the contributor to explain his point a bit further to clarify its relationship to the topic at hand.

- At the conclusion, summarize or ask a group member to summarize what has been said.

Excerpted with permission from: Iceland Defense Force (IDF) Overseas Diplomacy Program, Vol. II, "Overseas Diplomacy Training Program Manual." Center for Research and Education, Denver, Colorado, May 1976.

A SHORT GUIDE TO DESIGNING AND DOING AN EXPERIENTIAL EXERCISE

Claude Pepin

If you wish to use an experiential exercise, there are three
basic options available: (1) design a new one; (2) adapt an existing exercise to fit your purpose; or, (3) employ one which seems
well-suited to your particular situation. In any of the three cases,
the following questions and steps can serve as guidelines in preparing the exercise.

Observation Exercise: Student Group to Ghana

I. Consider the participants.

Questions	Facts and Assumptions
a. Who are they? How many? What are their backgrounds/ experiences?	a. Twenty U. S. college students going to Ghana for 3 months. Two have visited Africa. Five have traveled in Europe and Mexico. Thirteen have limited travel experience. All come from traditional university settings. None speaks Twi. Urban and suburban middle, upper middle class. Five black, 15 white. Major study fields varied.
b. What are their expectations?	b. Lecture or seminar on observations skills. Presentation of specific information about Ghana. Not expect-ing to see each other or themselves as resources for learning observation skills.
c. In what ways can their skills, energies and needs be utilized?	c. Make use of their enthusiasm as an energizing force; use the fact that two have been to W. Africa; use the fact that they have a wealth of observation experience among them, perhaps not consciously employed; use their hunger for culture-specific information about Ghana.

II. Clearly Define Your Purposes: If an exercise is to be an effective
    learning experience, it must be designed to bring about full
    participation.

152

Questions	Facts and Assumptions
a. Given the partici- pants, their program, their expectations and needs, what do you expect them to learn?	a. To understand that observations, judgements, and actions may be based totally upon past experiences in U. S. culture.
b. What are the key issues or significant points to be examined?	b. The difference between observation and judgement; relationship of personal experience to what one does/does not see, do,value; the fact that there is no single definition of any culture or nation state; that one's own set of observations, perceptions, judgements comprises a continually changing defin- ition of reality on which one acts each day; there are many ways to observe: seeing, listening, feeling, sensing, smelling, tasting, intuition; the importance of suspending final judge- ment by means of formulating low-level hypotheses which can be upgraded with new experience and observation; that improved skills in observation/per- ception/judgement will enhance one's effectiveness and enjoyment in another culture.

NOTE: The purpose of the exercise should be clearly defined. If a
participant experiences it fully, what will she/he learn? In addition
to the overall purpose, there are also sub-purposes or "learning points"
along the way. For example, in this case we have focused on the
influences of past experience upon observation, judgement and subsequent
action. A representative "learning point" which leads up to our
purpose could be defined as learning how past experience influences
judgement, observation, perception in new situations and in different
cultural contexts. Another "learning point" might be an examination of
these elements as preludes to appropriate action or inappropriate
action in our American context and in the Ghanian context.

III. Ways and Means.

Questions	Facts and Assumptions

a. What are alterna-
tive ways to accomplish
this purpose and those
learning points?
	a. -Discussions of selected readings
	   -Role play of a typical Ghanaian scene
	   -A series of slides about Ghanaian life
	   -A short film about Ghana
	   -Lecture by a Ghanaian guest
	   -An activity which requires partici-
	    pants to observe and to take action.

| b. How did I learn these things in my own life? | b. -Common experience of sharing an epidode or event with someone else and reaching two different conclusions
-The first time I am treated by a female physician
-My first exposure to sharp criticism of U. S. foreign policy by someone from another culture. |

At this state it might be more useful and productive to generate imaginative ideas to meet your purposes, rather than thinking of constraints and trying to design the exercises around them. Constraints can be applied too quickly to the seed of a creative idea. Try to keep in mind the learning points you have identified. The exercise you choose should ideally allow each participant the opportunity to relate to the experience in his or her individual way.

The following questions guide you in considering the relative merits of various exercises you might want to use:

1. How much time do we have for the exercise or activity and the discussion?
2. How much time do I have to prepare?
3. What resources do I have available to me (space, people, materials, etc.)?
4. What assumptions have I made about the participants, the materials, and other factors?
5. What questions will be useful and appropriate for discussion?
   Some questions appropriate for an observation exercise might be:
   -What did you observe?
   -Am I talking about observations or judgements?
   -Did other people observe the same things I did? Why or why not?
   -How did my assumptions influence what I observed?
   -What do I need to learn to "free-up" my observations from my personal biases or the limitations of my personal experience or knowledge?

Important parts of the discussion are identified by the open-ended questions asked by the facilitator to bring out the key learning points. Also important is the evaluation and feedback on the entire exercise, which will help everyone understand whether or not the original purposes of the exercise have been achieved.

From: Beyond Experience. Batchelder, Donald and Elizabeth G. Warner, eds. The Experiment Press, Brattleboro, Vermont, 1977. With permission.

THE PARABLE

An Introduction to Cultural Values[1]

Henry Holmes and Stephen Guild

Introduction. This is a useful exercise for

1. helping participants get acquainted with each other
2. demonstrating, through the discoveries they will make
   themselves, how their decisions are determined by
   cultural values
3. acquainting participants with specific cultural differences
   and similarities among other members of the group
4. stimulating awareness of problems in transmitting one's
   own ideas and listening to others'.

This sort of novel beginning also tends to provide a congenial
atmosphere which often leads to some laughter, informal conversation,
as well as cultural understanding. Participants are likely to pursue
their conversations after the session.

Facilities Needed. 1. Chalkboard and chalk 2. Paper and pencils
3. Comfortable seating arrangements, in which chairs can be moved into
small groups and 4. The size of the group is unimportant--from 10 to
as many as 100 people.

Time Required. About 25 minutes for the exercise itself.

Procedure. The leader tells a simple yet somewhat ambiguous
parable, in this case one involving 5 characters. He may draw stick
figures on the board as "illustrations" of the story. The behavior of
each of the characters is intended to suggest a number of different
values. After the parable each participant is asked to select, in
rank of order, the characters whose behavior he most approves; then
the large group is divided into groups of four or five to discuss

---

[1]This technique is the contribution of Sidney Simon, Professor
of Education at the University of Massachusetts.

individual choices. An open discussion follows, in which participants are asked to share on a voluntary basis what they have learned during the small group sessions.

   Steps to Follow. 1. The leader tells the following parable to the group, illustrating with rough drawings if he chooses:

   "Rosemary is a girl of about 21 years of age. For several months she has been engaged to a young man named--let's call him Geoffrey. The problem she faces is that between her and her betrothed there lies a river. No ordinary river mind you, but a deep, wide river infested with hungry crocodiles.

   "Rosemary ponders how she can cross the river. She thinks of a man she knows, who has a boat. We'll call him Sinbad. So she approaches Sinbad, asking him to take her across. He replies, 'Yes, I'll take you across if you'll spend the night with me.' Shocked at this offer, she turns to another acquaintance, a certain Frederick, and tells him her story. Frederick responds by saying, 'Yes, Rosemary, I understand your problem--but--it's your problem, not mine.' Rosemary decides to return to Sinbad, spend the night with him, and in the morning he takes her across the river.

   "Her reunion with Geoffrey is warm. But on the evening before they are to be married, Rosemary feels compelled to tell Geoffrey how she succeeded in getting across the river. Geoffrey responds by saying, 'I wouldn't marry you if you were the last woman on earth.'

   "Finally, at her wits' end, Rosemary turns to our last character, Dennis. Dennis listens to her story and says, 'Well, Rosemary, I don't love you . . . . but I will marry you.' And that's all we know of the story."

   2. The leader now asks each participant to write down on a piece of paper, in rank of order, the characters whose behavior he most approves, plus a sentence or two explaining his first choice.

   3. Next, participants are split into groups of four or five and asked to share--each with the others in his group--the choices he made. Not more than 10 - 15 minutes should be allowed for this discussion; its main purpose is to raise the issues, not to exhaust them.

   4. He asks, "Would anyone care to volunteer anything you learned as a result of the discussion you have just had--anything at all?" He should allow a short discussion to follow and call for a few other volunteers to share what they have learned.

   5. He may then ask the group, "Can anyone point to some place, some source within your own past where you learned the values that caused you to take the position that you did?" Participants will

probably have some difficulty with this question; no matter. It is intended to be a difficult question.

6. Next the leader says, "Now I would like you to ask yourselves--I don't want an answer on this one, just want you to consider--how many of you feel you could faithfully re-state, to the satisfaction of someone else in your small group, the point of view, the value being expressed by that person? Again, I don't want you to answer, just think about the question."

7. The leader may then summarize the session briefly, making the following points, preferably on chalkboard or newsprint:

a. Values come out of one's cultural background. They are difficult to track down to a particular source and are often part of a person's unconscious behavior.

b. Within any particular culture a person's values are usually very logical. They make sense in that culture.

c. For these reasons people should be very cautious about making moral judgement about other people's values.

d. If one really wants to understand someone else, one has to listen extremely well and really try to "get inside" the other person. This is the reason for the question, "How accurately do you think you could re-state someone else's opinion?" Those of you who would have to answer "not very" have some work to do.

e. What are some other areas in life where people's values differ?

f. Now that you are acquainted with some people from other cultures, you may want to investigate, directly with them, some of the values and beliefs which they prize the most.

8. If the participants keep a journal (which can be a useful aid to learning), they should be asked to record what they have learned during the session.

9. The leader should conclude the session almost as if it were the beginning, rather than the end, of a learning experience. One way to do this is simply to say that this is the end of the formal session and then join one of the small groups for conversation, rather than leave the room.

Excerpted from: A Manual of Teaching Techniques for Intercultural Education, University of Massachusetts, Amherst, 1971. (with permission)

SELECTION OF EXERCISES FOR SMALL GROUPS

Robert Kohls
Paula Barnak
Sandra Tijitendero
Jackie Segars

A WAY OF GETTING AT AMERICAN VALUES

Robert Kohls

Write on the blackboard:
Cleanliness is next to godliness.
Time is money.
A woman's place is in the home.
Little children should be seen and not heard.

Ask everyone in the group to take 10 to 15 minutes to write
down all the American axioms and proverbs they have heard over and
over again. (If any foreign students are in the group, have them
do the same for their country or countries.)

Then share and collect by writing on the blackboard.

Then, next to each axiom, determine (as a group) what value is
being taught.

Examples	Values
Cleanliness is next to godliness	Cleanliness
Time is money	Value of time thriftiness
A penny saved is a penny earned	Thriftiness
Birds of a feather flock together	Guilt through association
Don't cry over spilt milk	Practicality
Waste not; want not	Frugality
Early to bed, early to rise...	Diligence
God helps those who help themselves	Initiative
It's not whether you win or lose, but...	Good sportsmanship
A man's home is his castle	Privacy; property
No rest for the wicked	Guilt; work ethic
You've made your bed, now sleep in it	Responsibility

These are only a few, very random examples. The list is endless,
but the point has been made. With only a dozen or so axioms, you have
a pretty good list of American values being expressed.
You might then want to have the groups brainstorm other basic
American values which are still missing from our list.

159

REACHING CONSENSUS

J. Robert Kohls

1. Divide into smaller sub-groups (of 4 or 5)
2. Individually, indicate whether you "agree" or "disagree" with each statement provided below.
3. Then, going over each statement in order, check to see if anyone in your group disagrees with each one. If even one person disagrees, the group should change the wording so that the statement is acceptable, as reworded, with all members of the group.
4. You may not simply "agree to disagree." That's a cop-out.
5. Choose one member to record the revised statements.
6. Report orally. Ask each group to report on a couple of the statements. And ask for alternate revisions from other groups.
7. If time is limited it's a good idea to ask one or two of the sub-groups to start from the bottom of the list and work their way to the top, so that all statements will be covered.
8. The important advantage of such an exercise is not so much in the validity of the statements, per se, but in the discussions they spark.

STATEMENTS

1. The fact that America was able to place a man on the moon proves America's technological superiority.
2. Foreigners going to live in a new country should give up their foreign ways and adapt to the new country as quickly as possible.
3. Orientals do many things backwards.
4. Much of the world's population does not take enough initiative to develop themselves, therefore they remain "underdeveloped."
5. English should be accepted as the universal language of the world.
6. The Vietnamese do not place any value on human life. To them life is cheap.
7. Americans have been very generous in teaching other people how to do things the right way.
8. Primitive people have not yet reached the higher stages of civilization.
9. Minority members of any population should be expected to conform to the customs and values of the majority.
10. The sooner the whole world learns to do things the way we do, the sooner all the people of the world will be able to understand each other better.

"AS IF..." EXERCISE

Robert Kohls

Divide the group into pairs or triads, and assign each to consider in detail what a society would be like if it were based on one of the premises listed below. Allow 20 minutes, then regroup and report to the entire group, eliciting other comments as well.

What would a society be like IF it believed implicitly:
1. in reincarnation and karma
2. that all other people are infidels
3. that all events in the world are determined by Fate
4. a person's worth is determined solely by his/her "high"
5. in the passive approach to life as preferable to an action orientation
6. that certain ethnic or racial groups are intellectually inferior and emotionally immature
7. that old people were to be revered, honored and deferred to in all instances
8. that aesthetic values are of supreme importance and should be used to determine every major issue in life
9. that rights of groups are more important than those of the individual
10. that women are superior to men

Final points to be made at the end of the discussion:
1. There _are_ groups or societies which believe all of these premises and shape their lives around them.
2. And most of these premises are very "un-American" (i.e. except for #6, American society tends to be based on premises which are diametrically opposed to those listed above).

CROSS-CULTURAL ANALYSIS EXERCISE
Paula Barnak

Purpose

The cross-cultural analysis exercise is designed to help the participants begin focusing on differences between their own culture and the culture(s) they will be in contact with. One of the problems is that we take our culture for granted. Contrasting American cultural attitudes with those of another will help the participants learn not only about the new culture but also about their own, and that much of what they consider to be right or wrong, or "human nature," is actually culturally determined. With this understanding of cultural differences, it is much easier to achieve an openness to experience in one's approach to another culture.

Procedures

The exercise is first completed individually and then in small discussion groups (see instructions prefacing the Cross-Cultural Exercise).

At the conclusion of the group discussions, bring the participants together again for a summary discussion. Choose a number of concepts, and ask a member of each group:

- What is the basic American attitude toward (for example):

  - status, rank and education?
  - authority?
  - commitments?
  - family?
  - women?
  - change?
  - etc.

- What is the general attitude of the "Designated National" (i.e., the particular culture group you will be working with) toward these same concepts?

- What are some kinds of problems you feel could arise from the differences in the American and Designated National attitudes or positions in relation to these cultural dimensions or concepts?

- What actions might you take to resolve these problems or prevent them from developing?

You may find it helpful to summarize their perceptions by writing out on the flip chart the key concepts and attitudes that come out of this discussion. For example:

Concept	Attitude	Conflict Situation	Possible Action

162

Instructions for Individual Work

Working alone, study each of the cultural dimensions in the attached list. Then, using the nine-point scale:

1. Indicate where you feel the "typical" American position is on each dimension. (Mark in the upper row of each box.)

2. Indicate where you feel the position of the "typical" Designated National (i.e., the particular cultural group you will be working with) is on each dimension.

3. Indicate where you feel your position is on each dimension.

Group Instructions

When you have completed the individual assignments, meet in your designated discussion group and complete the following:

1. As a group, reach a consensus on the nine-point scale where you feel the typical American position is on each dimension. (Mark in the lower row of each box.)

2. Reach a consensus on the nine-point scale where you feel the typical Designated National position is on each dimension.

3. Describe in short, written statements, basic attitudes of the American and the Designated National under each concept. (Use a separate piece of paper.)

4. List the kinds of problems that you feel could arise from the differences and conflicts in the American and the Designated National positions on each dimension.

5. Indicate what action you might take to resolve these problems or prevent them from developing.

These answers will then be discussed in a summary session.

Note: In addition to your own culture-specific reading, as preparation for conducting this exercise, you may find it helpful to ask a National from the specific country involved (if possible) to complete the exercise and discuss the results with you.

Excerpted with permission from: Iceland Defense Force (IDF) Overseas Diplomacy Program, Vol. II, "Overseas Diplomacy Training Program Manual." Center for Research and Education, Denver, Colorado, May 1976.

CROSS-CULTURAL ANALYSIS

A

American
Designated
Host National
self

1. Attitude toward life:

Basically
good

Willing to sacrifice
individual for
welfare of group

1   2   3   4   5   6   7   8   9

2. Attitude toward science, technology, and machines:

Highly
valued

People more
important

1   2   3   4   5   6   7   8   9

3. Attitude toward time:

Present success
and satisfaction
important

Present success and
satisfaction not
important

1   2   3   4   5   6   7   8   9

4. Attitude toward achievement:

Goal and accomp-
lishment-oriented

Human relations-
oriented

1   2   3   4   5   6   7   8   9

5. Attitude toward work:

Work to
live

Live to
work

1   2   3   4   5   6   7   8   9

6. Attitude toward small group or family:

A man's only
real loyalty

Other relationships
more important

1   2   3   4   5   6   7   8   9

7. Attitude toward women:

Inferior
to men

Equal
to men

1   2   3   4   5   6   7   8   9

164

8. Style of communication:

Polite,   Frank,
vague,   open,
indirect   direct

   1   2   3   4   5   6   7   8   9

9. Attitude toward strangers:

Complete   Great hos-
distrust   pitality

   1   2   3   4   5   6   7   8   9

10. Attitude toward value of experience:

Learn   Mistakes should
by   be avoided at
mistakes   all costs

   1   2   3   4   5   6   7   8   9

11. Attitude toward "change":

Possible   Impossible
with effort   to achieve

   1   2   3   4   5   6   7   8   9

B

1. Attitude toward problem-solving:

Rational,   Instinctive,
logical   impulsive

    1   2   3   4   5   6   7   8   9

Man's   God's
duty   province

    1   2   3   4   5   6   7   8   9

2. Attitude toward status, rank, and education:

Based on   Earned by
heredity &   ability &
seniority   hard work

    1   2   3   4   5   6   7   8   9

3. Attitude toward control of one's environment:

Self-deter-   Fatalistic
mination

    1   2   3   4   5   6   7   8   9

4. Attitude toward relationship to others:

Meeting indi-   Group needs more
vidual needs   important than
important   individual needs

    1   2   3   4   5   6   7   8   9

5. Attitude toward authority:

Resentment,   Valued,
rebellion   respected

    1   2   3   4   5   6   7   8   9

6. Attitude toward meeting commitments (appointments,
   schedules, etc.):

Casual, little   Great
concern   concern

    1   2   3   4   5   6   7   8   9

(left margin, rotated)
American
Designated
Host National
Self

7. Attitude toward inefficiency and red tape:

A necessary   Unnecessary and
inconvenience   intolerable

   1   2   3   4   5   6   7   8   9

8. Concern for status:

Complete   Great
indifference   concern

   1   2   3   4   5   6   7   8   9

9. Attitude toward maintenance of classroom discipline:

Very strict,   Very permissive,
reliance on   reliance on stu-
punishment   dent responsibility

   1   2   3   4   5   6   7   8   9

10. Attitude toward responsibility:

Self-directed,   Other-directed,
takes initiative   waits for orders

   1   2   3   4   5   6   7   8   9

167

<u>PROVERBS</u>

Sandra Tjitendero

    Although we all know a proverb when we hear one, it is difficult to define the term precisely. The introduction of a specific culture can include a study of its proverbs: what they are and what purposes they serve in communication of attitudes, values, and beliefs. Proverbs can be defined as "short, pithy epigrammatic statements which set forth a general well-known truth. When viewed as part of a communicative act, they are vehicles for sending messages about opinions, feelings, manners or customs of a people. They serve as witnesses to social, political, ethical and religious patterns of thinking and behaving.

    Proverbs are characterized by a touch of the fanciful in their unique turn of a phrase, the unusual use of a word, or perhaps a specific rythm. Many are paradoxical, or antithetical, while others are strongly metaphorical. Here in a workshop format, we are concerned with how to use proverbs to get at underlying cultural assumptions. We can examine proverbs for their exaggeration of attitudes commonly held by a cultural group. Hyperbole, personification, and alliteration are common attributes of the proverb which give us an unforgettable phrase or kernel of thought. Each proverbial statement has a quality of permanence in the culture and recurs in its folk lore.

    Give participants a sheet of paper containing the following proverbs:
1.   "You got eyes to see and wisdom not to see."
2.   "Muddy roads call the mile post a liar."
3.   "Every bell ain't a dinner bell."
4.   "A mule can tote so much goodness in his face that he don't have none left for his hind legs."
5.   "The graveyard is the cheapest boarding house."

    For each of the above proverbs, choose a phrase in your own language which approximates the meaning of the proverb. Use familiar language, and symbols, for example: "Kumquats are both sweet and sour," if you aren't familiar or comfortable with "kumquats," substitute "oranges."

    What does the original proverb mean? What is its message?

    What does the proverb indicate to you about the culture? Can you generalize about it, whether it is traditional, rural, submissive, dominant, happy-go-lucky, cautious, etc.?

    What are the dominant values of the culture?

    Think of some parallel proverbs from your own culture. Convey a similar message if you can. If you cannot, why not? For example, "For the turtle to make progress, it must stick its neck out," is similar to "To learn to swim, you must first get your toes wet." The message is similar, the symbols are slightly different.

Try to identify the culture from which all five examples are
drawn.   What type of culture do you think it is, and some reasons why
you characterize it that way...elaborate.

At the end of the exercise, the trainer reveals that the culture
we are looking at is AfroAmerican Slave - these are real examples of
proverbs taken from the folk literature.

The first example, "You got eyes to see and wisdom not to see,"
is pointing to the slave culture's accurate perception of what goes on
around the people, but the sense not to "see" or acknowledge the
reality.   Emphasis is placed on not knowing something which would
upset you.

In the next example, the muddy roads are relatively impassable,
therefore the person traveling them cannot count on the mile posts
to gauge how long his journey will take.   We can tell this is a rural
culture, and that its people are used to translating signals into
their own particular knowledge about dealing with nature.

Number three indicates frequent conflicts between the dinner bell,
a safe cue, and the bell calling slaves in from the fields, sometimes a
warning of imminent danger.   Again, the rural culture is reflected in
the image of the bell.

The mule often looks like he will be a kind and helpful farm
animal, but his legs still can kick you or refuse to budge - so don't
be deceived by appearances.   Again, an agricultural culture is
reflected in the imagery, and a realism born of knowing the environment
and what you can expect.

The graveyard, in the last example, is escape from the troubles
of a hard life - so don't worry about death - death is a kind of
freedom for the slave, rest from all the hard times.

CONCERN CENSUS

Jackie Segars

1. Tape large sheet of paper on nearby visible wall.

2. If group is small (10 or less), operate as one group. If group
   is larger, split into 2 smaller groups and ask one person in
   each to take notes verbatim of members' contributions.

3. Begin by saying something like the following:
   We have all come to this special course with a lot of different
   feelings and concerns related to our abilities and/or inabilities
   to relate to others across cultural lines. Some of us have
   particular concerns in mind which we would like to resolve;
   others have interests which they would like to explore. We are
   going to have a concern census in order that we might share these
   concerns or interests as a group, record them on the large sheet
   of paper so that we might develop a profile of those thoughts
   which are uppermost in our group's mind, and attempt to deal
   with them as a group.

4. If in one group, give them one minute to think of their concerns
   silently; ask for them to volunteer their concerns which you will
   record VERBATIM on the large paper on the wall.

5. If in 2 or more smaller groups, ask them to think silently for
   one minute then each person tell the "recorder" in his/her group
   to record VERBATIM the concern; recorders then go to the large
   sheet of paper and record their small group's contributions.

6. It is important not to attempt to resolve or comment on the
   concerns at this point, only to gather them and share them without
   imposing a value system on them.

7. Regroup into one group.

8. Explain that you now have a Concern Profile of your group which
   gives it an identity and an initial direction to pursue.

9. Ask them to look for trends, patterns of feeling, the diversity of
   purposes for being in the course.

CHAPTER X

AREA-SPECIFIC TRAINING

171

CONCEPTUAL MODEL FOR AREA STUDIES

Robert Kohls

The attached model for developing complete coverage in producing
area studies material was originally prepared for use in Peace Corps
training projects for Korea, but it has been revised and expanded
considerably since then. It is felt, while it applies specifically to
Korea, that it could be used as a model for the development of area
studies materials for other countries as well. The three separate
sections described below make it possible not only to systematically
organize a huge body of disparate materials, but also to spot any
obvious omissions rather easily, especially when the outline is checked
over by several other people who are familiar with the culture under
consideration.
    The material is divided into:
1)   factual information about the country;
2)   information about the attitudes of the people of the target
      country (uninfluenced by the outside world); and,
3)   a discussion of specific problems the foreigner who goes to
      that country is likely to encounter.

Section I   Briefings (Factual Background Information)
    This category contains the kind of factual information that can
be compiled by anyone (whether he has ever visited the country or not)
given a couple of weeks' time and a good resource library. Although
all of the sub- headings would be entirely different for any other
country, the major headings under this section of the Korea outline
(e.g. History, Religion and Philosophy, Economics and Industry, Politics
and Government,) can probably be lifted in toto and used as a guide
for compiling this kind of background information for any country.
    Section I contains the least important type of information to be
given to the trainees, since it is possible for any intelligent person
to gather it on his own. It is the easiest section to compile, and
contains the kind of material which is usually given through lectures,
not necessarily because the lecture has proven to be very effective,
but because it is difficult to find a more exciting format to present the
information than through either a lecture, or a mimeographed handout,
or reading assignments using a syllabus to guide the information-
gathering reading.
    The factual background information provided in this section
covers the broad areas that are pertinent to the study of any culture:
history, human and natural resources, family and social structure,
religion, philosophy, education, fine arts and cultural achievements,

172

economics and industry, politics and government, medicine, science
and sports and games.

Section II Profile Information, Personality Traits, Attitudes,
           Behavior, Value Systems, and Traditional Thought Patterns

This section is by far the most difficult to formulate, and it is
very doubtful that the headings or sub-headings used for Korea would
be of any use whatsoever in preparing material for a different culture.
This is the section which describes the host country national; it is
the kind of information which is not only difficult to formulate but
sometimes even embarrassing to write down, because it begins to
resemble the stereotypes and prejudices which liberal-minded people
prefer to avoid rather than make concrete by putting them into words
and sentences. It is the sort of information no scholar would be willing
to publish under his name. Because of its nature, however, it becomes
increasingly more valuable than the first section to somehow present
to the trainees.

This section can only be prepared by someone extremely conversant
with the culture concerned. It should, also, be formulated by someone
who is sympathetic, sensitive, and as objective as humanly possible.
He should be aware of the probable cultural reasons behind the customs
themselves. There are few books to refer to for help; he can only
call upon his experiences, hopefully over many years, in-country.
The information in this category should be checked and double-checked
by as many authorities as possible (including some nationals in the
later stages of its development) for their corrections and the addition
of their valuable suggestions.

Section III Integration Problems Faced by Foreigners

The preceding section dealt with the host country national as he
is within his own country and with little or no influence from other
countries. This division describes some of the problems an American
is likely to run into when faced with the situation he finds in the
host country. These are problems, it should be pointed out, which
would not exist in the country were it not for the presence of the
foreigner there. They cannot, then, be blamed on the country or on
the host country nationals (as is so often done) but rather on the
contrasting enculturation the foreigner brings with him. These are
truly the cross-cultural concerns of area studies. These entries will
vary considerably for each country, the Korean examples probably not
serving as relevant models for any other country.

This material is the most useful in preparing a person to go to
another country, and should definitely be prepared by an American who
has had experience living in the target country and a great deal of
cross-cultural experience in general.

The material covered in sections II and III can be advantageously
presented by using a technique that is much more effective than the
traditional lecture method. In a "co-teaching" format, two specialists
on the target culture converse informally in front of the training body,
in a guided (i.e. following an outline sketch) yet spontaneous dis-
course concerning each of the topics under consideration. Incompatible
and controversial opinions, where they exist, should be encouraged,

173

for there often is more than one "answer" to any subject. Again, it
is essential that both experts be sympathetic to the target culture and
to its nationals so that the differences mentioned above would not be
indicative of a pro-American or anti-target country bias.
    While prepared specifically for Korea, it is felt that the model
could, with a little imagination and more checking and rechecking,
be applied to the needs of any country as a guide to the development of
relevant area studies materials.

                  AREA STUDIES COVERAGE FOR KOREA

Section I   Briefings (Factual Background Information)

      A.   History

           Symbolism of Korean Flag; National Anthem; National Flower
           Origin of Koreans
           Prehistoric Period
           Three Kingdoms Period (Koguryo, Paekje, and Old Silla)
           United Silla Period
           Koryŏ Dynasty
           Lee (Yi/I-jo) Dynasty
           Period of Japanese Domination
           Modern Period

      B.   Human and Natural Resources and Facilities

           Geography; Topography
           Climate; Seasons
           Flora and Fauna
           Natural Resources
           Population
           Communications Systems
           Mass Communication Media
           Transportation

      C.   Family and Social Structure

           Chokbo (Lineage) System
           Kinship Groups
           Extended Family System
           Roles of Family Members
           Social Classes
           Servants
           Ancestor Worship
           Rural Life cf. City Life

      D.   Religion, Philosophy and Beliefs
           Taeguk (Ŭm-Yang) Symbolism
           Shamanism (and Mudang)
           Tan'gun Legan
           Buddhism
           Neo-Confucianism

                              174

Tonghak Movement (Chondo'gyo)
Real Learning School (Silhakpa)
Christianity in Korea
Fortune Telling and Geomancy

E. Education

Traditional (Confucian) Educational Concepts
Responsibilities of School; Responsibilities of Home
Korean School System (various levels)

F. Fine Arts and Cultural Achievements

Painting
Calligraphy
Sculpture
"Minor Arts" (e.g. Ceramics, Lacquerware, Furniture)
Crafts (Folk arts)
Architecture
Music (including Court Music and Traditional Musical
        Instruments)
Dance (including Farmer's Dance)
Drama and Masked Drama
Literature
Poetry (including Sijo)
Korean Inventions and Achievements

G. Korean Language

Possible Origin and Links
Characteristics
Chinese Characters
Han'gŭl Alphabet

H. Economics and Industry

Principal Industries
Export/Import
Foreign Import
Foreign Investment
"Kye" System
Cottage Industries
Government Monopolies
Five-Year Plans
Mondernization
Vietnam's Effect on Korean Economy
U.N., USOM (AID),and KAVA (Voluntary Agencies)
Traditions Maintained in Rural Korea
Effects of Modernization ("Westernization") in Large
        Urban Areas
Agriculture
Fishing
Local Market Day System

I. Politics and Government

    Korean-Japanese Relations
    North and South Korea
    Student Demonstrations
    Military Coup
    Attitude re: Communism
    Political Parties
    Government Organization (Central and Local)
    Korean CIA
    Police System
    U.S. Military Involvement
    Korean Military Strength
    Korean Involvement in Vietman

J. Medicine

    Han Yak
    Acapuncture and Moxabustion
    Ginseng
    Western Medicine

K. Sports and Games

    Native Sports (Tangsu, Taekwando, Korean Wrestling, Archery)
    Modern World Sports
    Traditional Korean Games

Section II Profile Information, Korean Personality Traits, Attitudes, Behavioral Characteristics, Value Systems, and Traditional Thought Patterns

A. People Oriented vs. Material (or Fact; or Progress) Oriented

    Sincerity
    "Face" and "Kibun"
    Attitudes re: Age
    Attitudes re: Superiors
        "Assumed Humility"
        Social Connotations of the Language
    Ways of Expressing Emotions

B. Relationships Between Parties (and Chain of Command)

    With Parents
    With Peers
    Husband and Wife
    Boy and Girl Relationships
    Teacher and Students
    Employer and Employee
    Householder and Servant
    Influence of Confucianism
    Importance of Ceremony
    Indirect Communication
    Ignoring Unpleasant Things
    Introductions
    Importance of Proper Posture

176

C. In-Group Affiliations

Korean Society a Collection of Groups
Group Allegiance
Use of Personal Names
Generosity and Sharing
Ideas of ownership and Property (including Borrowing)
Privacy

D. Attitudes Toward the Out-Groups

Lack of Concern for Outsiders
Fights Require Arbitrators
Attitudes Toward the Unfortunate
Attitudes Toward Thieves, Beggars, and Criminals
Attitudes re: Wealth and the Wealthy
Attitudes Toward Women
Attitudes Toward Children
Traditional Stereotypes of Provincial Characteristics
Attitudes Toward Foreigners
Attitudes Toward Public Service
Attitudes Toward Race

E. Attitudinal Concepts

Effects of Confucianism
Active vs. Passive
Concepts of Space
Concepts of Time (and Punctuality)
        Patience
        Reverence for the Past
        Cyclical Sequence Rather than Progressive
Attitude Toward Material and Spiritual Concerns
Attitude Toward Scholars and Education
Attitude Toward Labor
Attitude Toward Individuality
Attitude Toward Independence

F. Paths to Success (How to Get Ahead)

Requests for Favors
Dependence on Relatives and In-Group Members
        "Back"
Attitudes Toward Help
        Giver and Receiver
Use of Gifts Toward Expecting Favors in Return
Ways of Receiving Gifts
Contracts and Loans
Bribery and Graft
Practice of "Tipping" Permanently-Employed Help

G. Enduring Hardships, Sadness, and Suffering

Ability to Adjust to Present Situation
Strong Support from In-Group Members
Fatalistic Attitude
Attitude re: Hunger

177

H.   Korean Sense of Humor

   Often Bawdy
   Ability to Make Own Entertainment
   Laugh Often Used to Cover Embarrassment

I   Attitudes re: Love, Dating, Marriage, Sex

   Wives
   Concubines
   Kisaeng
   Prostitutes

J.   Customs, Manners, and Etiquette

   Korean Names and Titles
   Seals cf. Signatures
   Meeting Etiquette(Types of Bows)
   Smoking and Drinking Etiquette
   Ways of Sitting
   Necessity to be Urged Several Times to Enter, Sit, Eat, etc.
   Home and Social Life
   Physical Contact Between Same Sex
   Food
   Clothing
   Houses
   Birthday Customs
        Sixty-First Birthday Celebration (Hwan Gahp)
   Marriage Customs
        Arranged Marriages
   Holidays
        Lunar Calendar
        Oriental Zodiac

Section III Integration Problems Faced by Foreigners

   A.   Foreigners as an "Un-Person" (Sang Nom)

   B.   General Staring and Rudeness on Streets

   C.   Passive Resistance Rather than Disagreement or Refusal

   D.   Americans' Reactions to Extreme Poverty and Beggars

   E.   Korean Reactions to American Affluence

   F.   Reactions to Theft, Bribery, and Dishonesty

   G.   Cleanliness and Sanitation

   H.   Health Problems

   I.   Reaction to Strange Smells

   J.   Difficulties with Adjusting to Food

   K.   Learning to Share

   L.   Lack of Privacy

178

UPDATE: SAUDI ARABIA

Alison R. Lanier

(This is the Table of Contents of a volume on Saudi Arabia published by the
Overseas Briefing Associates. The editors feel it constitutes an excellent
outline of the kind of information which should be included in culture-
specific cross-cultural training.)

Section I. BACKGROUND

Section II. DOING BUSINESS WITH SAUDIS

A. The People

B. Business Mechanics

181

E. Food Precautions

Section IX: LEISURE ACTIVITIES

Section X. MAJOR PLACES OF INTEREST

Section XI. SOURCES OF INFORMATION